Copyright © 2020 by Esther Wright - All rights reserved.

The content contained within this book may not be reproduced without direct written permission from the author or the publisher. any blame or legal responsibility be held against the publisher, or author, for any damages, reparation, or monetary loss due to the information contained within this book, either directly or indirectly.This book is copyright protected. It is only for personal use. You cannot amend, distribute, sell, use, quote or paraphrase any part, or the content within this book, without the consent of the author or publisher.

Please note the information contained within this document is for educational and entertainment purposes only. All effort has been executed to present accurate, up to date, reliable, complete information. No warranties of any kind are declared or implied. Readers acknowledge that the author is not engaged in the rendering of legal, financial, medical, or professional advice. The content within this book has been derived from various sources. Please consult a licensed professional before attempting any techniques outlined in this book.

By reading this document, the reader agrees that under no circumstances is the author responsible for any losses, direct or indirect, that are incurred as a result of the use of the information contained within this document, including, but not limited to, errors, omissions, or inaccuracies.

CONTENTS

INTRODUCTION 9
    Things You Need to Know About Your Zojirushi Bread Machine 9
    How to Store Your Bread 12

SPICE, NUT & HERB BREAD 13
    1. Seeded Bread 13
    2. Molasses Candied-ginger Bread 13
    3. Orange Almond Bacon Bread 13
    4. Garlic, Herb, And Cheese Bread 13
    5. Italian Pine Nut Bread 14
    6. Caramelized Onion Bread 14
    7. Honeyed Bulgur Bread 14
    8. Pesto Nut Bread 14
    9. French Herb Bread 15
    10. Fragrant Cardamom Bread 15
    11. Tuscan Herb Bread 15
    12. Mix Seed Raisin Bread 16
    13. Garlic Herb Bread 16
    14. Cheese Herb Bread 16
    15. Cardamom Cranberry Bread 16
    16. Chocolate Mint Bread 17
    17. Healthy Basil Whole Wheat Bread 17
    18. Pumpkin Coconut Almond Bread 17
    19. Sesame French Bread 17
    20. Raisin Seed Bread 18
    21. Herb And Garlic Cream Cheese Bread 18
    22. Herbed Pesto Bread 18
    23. Grain, Seed And Nut Bread 19
    24. Rosemary Cranberry Pecan Bread 19
    25. Onion Bacon Bread 19
    26. Basic Pecan Bread 20
    27. Delicious Cranberry Bread 20
    28. Market Seed Bread 20
    29. Pistachio Cherry Bread 21
    30. Cinnamon Bread 21
    31. Oatmeal Seed Bread 22
    32. Seed Bread 22
    33. Coffee Raisin Bread 22
    34. Almond Milk Bread 23
    35. Lavender Buttermilk Bread 23
    36. Olive Bread 23
    37. Spicy Cajun Bread 24
    38. Pumpkin Cinnamon Bread 24
    39. Cajun Bread 24
    40. Aromatic Lavender Bread 24
    41. Cracked Black Pepper Bread 25
    42. Whole-wheat Seed Bread 25
    43. Semolina Bread 25

44. Whole Wheat Raisin Bread 26
45. Pumpkin Pie Spice Bread 26
46. Oatmeal Sunflower Bread 26
47. Fragrant Herb Bread 27
48. Anise Lemon Bread 27
49. Macadamia Bread 27
50. Dilly Onion Bread 27
51. Turmeric Bread 28

FRUIT AND VEGETABLE BREAD 29
52. Fruit Raisin Bread 29
53. Fresh Blueberry Bread 29
54. Garlic Olive Bread 29
55. Garlic Onion Pepper Bread 30
56. Honey Banana Bread 30
57. Spice Peach Bread 30
58. Blueberry-basil Loaf 31
59. Cranberry & Golden Raisin Bread 31
60. Gluten-free Cinnamon Raisin Bread 32
61. Strawberry Oat Bread 32
62. Chocolate-pistachio Bread 32
63. Blueberry Bread 33
64. Oatmeal-streusel Bread 33
65. Mushroom Leek Bread 33
66. Poppy Seed–lemon Bread 34
67. Beetroot Bread 34
68. Onion Chive Bread 34
69. Basil Tomato Bread 35
70. Apple-fig Bread With Honey Glaze 35
71. Plum Orange Bread 35
72. Blueberries 'n Orange Bread 36
73. Cranberry Honey Bread 36
74. Raisin Candied Fruit Bread 37
75. Gluten-free Glazed Lemon-pecan Bread 37
76. Squash Carrot Bread 38
77. Monkey Bread 38
78. Brown Sugar Date Nut Swirl Bread 38
79. Zucchini Spice Bread 39
80. Perfect Sweet Potato Bread 39
81. Confetti Bread 40
82. Savory Onion Bread 40
83. Black Olive Bread 40
84. Yeasted Carrot Bread 41
85. Ginger-topped Pumpkin Bread 41
86. Delicious Apple Bread 41
87. Zucchini Bread 42
88. Olive Rosemary Bread 42
89. Sauerkraut Rye Bread 42
90. Honey Potato Flakes Bread 42

91. Cinnamon Pull-apart Bread 43
92. Tomato Herb Bread 43
93. Carrot Coriander Bread 44
94. Potato Honey Bread 44
95. Savory Sweet Potato Pan Bread 44
96. Pineapple Carrot Bread 45
97. Blueberry Honey Bread 45
98. Cinnamon Raisin Breadsticks 45
99. Zucchini Bread 46
100. Australian Vegetable Bread 46
101. Light Corn Bread 46
102. Cinnamon Apple Bread 47
103. Lemon-lime Blueberry Bread 47

CLASSIC DAILY BREAD 48
104. Whole Wheat Sunflower Bread 48
105. Garlic Pepperoni Bread 48
106. Oat Molasses Bread 48
107. Banana Bread 49
108. Citrus And Walnut Bread 49
109. Onion Bread 49
110. Bread Machine Bread 50
111. Flaxseed Milk Bread 50
112. Multigrain Honey Bread 50
113. Classic Corn Bread 51
114. 10 Minute Rosemary Bread 51
115. Cranberry Walnut Bread 51
116. Classic White Bread Ii 52
117. French Crusty Loaf Bread 52
118. Julekake 53
119. Cinnamon Rolls 53
120. Pumpernickel Bread 53
121. Buttermilk Bread 54
122. Classic Dark Bread 54
123. Pizza Rolls 55
124. Garlic Cheese Pull-apart Rolls 55
125. Rosemary Focaccia Bread 56
126. Lemon Cake 56
127. Fat-free Whole Wheat Bread 56
128. Basic Seed Bread 57
129. Pumpkin Spice Cake 57
130. Cinnamon Pecan Coffee Cake 57
131. Honey Pound Cake 58
132. Oat Bran Molasses Bread 58
133. Pepperoni Bread 58
134. Honey Nut Bread 58
135. Blue Cheese Bread 59
136. Oat Quinoa Bread 59
137. Rye Bread 59

138. Savory Bread Maker Rolls ... 60
139. Italian Easter Cake ... 60
140. Honey Sunflower Bread ... 60
141. Whole Wheat Corn Bread ... 61
142. Rainbow Swirl Cake ... 61
143. Christmas Bread ... 62
144. Apple Pecan Cinnamon Rolls ... 62
145. Coffee Rye Bread ... 63
146. Classic White Sandwich Bread ... 63
147. Baguette Style French Bread ... 63
148. Panettone ... 64
149. German Butter Cake ... 64
150. Donuts ... 65
151. Chocolate Chip Bread ... 65
152. Lemon Blueberry Quick Bread ... 65
153. Parsley And Chive Pull-apart Rolls ... 66
154. Oat Bran Nutmeg Bread ... 66
155. Chocolate Coffee Bread ... 67

BASIC BREAD ... **68**

156. Hawaiian Sandwich Bread ... 68
157. Coconut Flour Bread ... 68
158. Perfect Sandwich Bread ... 68
159. Vegan White Bread ... 68
160. Warm Spiced Pumpkin Bread ... 68
161. Extra Buttery White Bread ... 69
162. Oatmeal Walnut Bread ... 69
163. Luscious White Bread ... 69
164. Homemade Hot Dog And Hamburger Buns ... 70
165. Autumn Treasures Loaf ... 70
166. Vegan Cinnamon Raisin Bread ... 70
167. Traditional Italian Bread ... 71
168. Perfect Cocoa Bread ... 71
169. Honey Whole-wheat Sandwich Bread ... 71
170. Black Forest Loaf ... 71
171. Anadama Bread ... 72
172. Everyday White Bread ... 72
173. English Muffin Bread ... 72
174. Italian Restaurant Style Breadsticks ... 72
175. Almond Flour Bread ... 73
176. Banana Lemon Loaf ... 73
177. Simple White Bread ... 73
178. Whole Wheat Rolls ... 74
179. 100 Percent Whole-wheat Bread ... 74
180. Italian White Bread ... 74
181. Classic White Bread I ... 75
182. Friendship Bread ... 75
183. Cracked Wheat Bread ... 75
184. Pumpernickel Bread 3 ... 76

185. Mustard Sour Cream Bread 76
186. Golden Raisin Bread 76
187. Healthy Whole Wheat Bread 77
188. Bagels 77
189. Low-carb Multigrain Bread 77
190. Gluten-free White Bread 78
191. Mediterranean Semolina Bread 78
192. Golden Corn Bread 78
193. Homemade Wonderful Bread 78
194. Soft Sandwich Bread 79
195. Multigrain Olive Oil White Bread 79
196. Chocolate Chip Banana Bread 79
197. Gluten-free Simple Sandwich Bread 80
198. Slider Buns 80
199. Beer Bread 80
200. Rice Flour Rice Bread 81
201. Flax Bread 81
202. Dark Rye Bread 81
203. Whole Wheat Breakfast Bread 81
204. Molasses Wheat Bread 82
205. Peasant Bread 82
206. Mom's White Bread 82

CHEESE & SWEET BREAD **83**
207. Wine And Cheese Bread 83
208. Cheese Jalapeno Bread 83
209. Cocoa Banana Bread 83
210. Buttery Sweet Bread 83
211. Apple Butter Bread 84
212. Oregano Cheese Bread 84
213. Crunchy Wheat-and-honey Twist 84
214. Date And Nut Bread 85
215. Italian Cheese Bread 85
216. Hot Cross Buns 85
217. Delicious Sour Cream Bread 86
218. Parmesan Cheddar Bread 86
219. Mozzarella Cheese And Salami Loaf 86
220. Cinnamon Rum Bread 87
221. Easy Donuts 87
222. Prosciutto Parmesan Breadsticks 88
223. Parsley Garlic Bread 88
224. Allspice Currant Bread 88
225. Savory Cheddar Cheese Bread 89
226. Cashew Butter/peanut Butter Bread 89
227. Ricotta Bread 89
228. Chocolate Orange Bread 90
229. Cheesy Chipotle Bread 90
230. Chocolate Chip Peanut Butter Banana Bread 90
231. Italian Herb Cheese Bread 91

232. Cottage Cheese And Chive Bread 91
233. Sugared Doughnuts 91
234. Parmesan Tomato Basil Bread 92
235. Cream Cheese Bread 92
236. Hawaiian Sweet Bread 92
237. Delicious Italian Cheese Bread 92
238. Cinnamon Cranberry Bread 93
239. Blue Cheese Bread 93
240. Jalapeño Corn Bread 93
241. Apricot–cream Cheese Ring 93
242. Romano Oregano Bread 94
243. Garlic Parmesan Bread 94
244. Choco Chip Pumpkin Bread 95
245. Onion, Garlic, Cheese Bread 95
246. Cinnamon Bread 95
247. Chocolate Oatmeal Banana Bread 95
248. Milk Sweet Bread 96
249. Olive And Cheddar Loaf 96
250. Crusty Honey Bread 96
251. Swedish Coffee Bread 97
252. Cottage Cheese Bread 97
253. Honey Granola Bread 97
254. Rich Cheddar Bread 98
255. Simple Cottage Cheese Bread 98
256. Sweet Applesauce Bread 98
257. Saffron And Tomato Bread 99
258. Fruit Bread 99

BREAD FROM AROUND THE WORLD **100**
259. White Chocolate Bread 100
260. Corn Poppy Seeds Sour Cream Bread 100
261. Greek Bread 100
262. Spicy Bread 100
263. European Black Bread 101
264. Seeded Whole Wheat Bread 101
265. Fluffy Paleo Bread 101
266. Peanut Butter And Jelly Bread 102
267. Quick Bake Italian Bread 102
268. Portuguese Sweet Bread 102
269. Bacon And Cheese Bread 102
270. Italian Panettone 103
271. Peanut Butter Cookies 103
272. Country-styled White Bread 103
273. Simple Dark Rye Bread 104
274. Oatmeal Bread 104
275. Amish Wheat Bread 104
276. Raisin Bread 105
277. Spiced Jalapeno Cheese Bread 105
278. Keto Breadsticks 105

279. Paleo And Dairy-free Bread 106
280. Russian Black Bread 106
281. Classic French Bread 106
282. Thin Crust Pizza Dough 107
283. Low-carb Zucchini Loaf 107
284. Italian Parmesan Bread 107
285. Milk White Bread 107
286. Puri Bread 108
287. Sausage Bread 108
288. Ciabatta 108
289. Syrian Bread 109
290. Corn Bread 109
291. Vanilla Milk Bread 109
292. Low-carb Apple Bread 110
293. Soft Pretzels 110
294. Pita Bread 110
295. German Pumpernickel Bread 111
296. Fiji Sweet Potato Bread 111
297. Pita Bread With Black Cumin 111
298. Gluten-free Bread 111
299. Coffee Cake 112
300. Argentine Chimichurri Bread 112

INTRODUCTION

Things You Need to Know About Your Zojirushi Bread Machine

The Advantages of the Zojirushi Bread Machine
Owning a bread machine is a great advantage for your busy lifestyle as it not only saves time in the kitchen but also makes your life better in many ways.

Fresh Bread Anytime
Traditional oven baking is not so much a single task as a series of steps. It requires careful planning to get baked bread out of your oven. Of course, you can purchase bread from your local bakery, but it's not always freshly baked. With a bread machine, you do not have to plan in advance as all you need to do is add the ingredients and start the machine. You can enjoy freshly baked bread anytime you want it.

Ingredient Freedom
You don't have any choice as to the ingredients in commercially available bread. With a bread machine, you can customize the taste and texture of your bread because you have the freedom to add your favorite fruits, spices, herbs, cheese, and so on and enjoy your choice of flavors.

Effortless and Clutterless
Traditional bread-making makes lots of mess with all the mixing and kneading. A bread machine creates no mess at all, as everything from mixing to baking is done within the bread pan.

Healthy and Economical
When you add up the cost of store-bought bread over the years, a bread machine is a much more economical choice. More importantly, it is a smart way to enjoy freshly baked bread with healthy ingredients as you can choose the flour and everything else that goes into it.

Common FAQs for Using Your Zojirushi Bread Machine
Bread making problems appear all the time. Once you've been baking for a while and gained experience, you can often tell if the dough is right by how it responds to touch and how it feels, or even by just looking at it. But, in the beginning, when things don't work out, it can be quite complicated to figure out what went wrong. Of course, these problems can be solved quite simply, and we all know how much the experience gives us – but this is the age of information, so before having to encounter all of the results caused by such problems, you can just let me fill you in on some of them and advise you how to avoid them:

Problem one: My dough isn't rising.
Solution: A lot of people think the dough won't rise unless they leave it somewhere really warm for several hours. In reality, you don't need anything special for the dough to rise. I always use instant yeast as it is more reliable, then normal cold water. If it doesn't grow, it might be because of the yeast – fresh yeast can be weak. Also, if you use water that is too hot or add certain acidic ingredients and certain spices like pepper and lemon powder, it can kill your yeast.

Problem two: I feel I need to increase my dough's rise.
Solution: You don't need an exquisite proving drawer to get a good result, generally, if you want to boost, you can just warm it up a little bit. Water that's around 35°C will give the dough an instant boost. You can even pop the dough in a cold oven and put a reading lamp or something similar above it – the heat from the bulb can give it a nice boost. You can also try adding an extra pinch of sugar as it will give the yeast more to feed on.

Problem three: My finished loaf is kinda heavy and soggy.
Solution: There are actually a few things that can cause this, but it mainly happens because of the way in which the bread has been baked. I often recommend people to go and buy a cheap, marble cutting board to use as a baking stone. These boards usually come in the perfect size, so you can avoid buying an expensive baking stone. Preheat it in the oven, at the 460-500°F, shape your loaf on a piece of non-stick paper, and then, when it's proved, carefully put it straight onto the hot stone and lower the temperature of the oven down to 180-200°C. Most loaves turn out soggy at the bottom because they haven't got the required heat, but this is how you can simulate that.

Problem four: When I'm kneading the dough, it sticks to the work surface and my hands.
Solution: The solution strictly depends on what bread you're making. Things like, for example, focaccia have a runny dough that makes it bubbly. A normal loaf becomes less gluey the more you knead it - at first, the dough is always wet and sticky, but once you've kneaded it for five to six minutes, it becomes less so and becomes glossy as it develops a coat, which is the gluten forming. After a couple more minutes of kneading, you will get to a point where your hands become cleaner through the kneading motion, as the dough isn't sticky anymore. If it seems, like reaching this point is taking too long, just give it another sprinkle of flour.

Problem five: I feel like my dough has over proved, but I can't really tell.
Solution: There is not one, but a couple of things that can cause over proving. Usually, it happens because the yeast sat for too long. It may not necessarily be exhausted, but the air bubbles could become too big, or it may have lost its structure. Generally, if you leave it to prove for over 40 minutes, it goes into an over proved state, which won't give you a good loaf. If you want to prevent that, don't let the dough double – once it has grown by roughly two thirds, it's already good to go in the oven as it will continue growing in there, and you will get what's called the 'oven spring.' One working way to tell whether your dough has proved enough or not is by pressing it with your finger. It should have a spring back feedback and return to its shape quickly, but not too much - if it springs back really quickly, it probably means that it started to overprove and has taken too much air inside.

Problem six: My free-form/formless loaf rises bakes unevenly.
Solution: You want to create a skin on your loaf to stop this from happening. If you were making, for example, a round loaf of bread, you need to put some flour on your hands, tip out your proved dough, and then do kind of a tucking and spinning action, so you're continually rotating the dough and tucking it under itself. In the process, it will start to develop a really tight skin, becoming almost like a nice tight football. The fact you have created that surface tension will give you a perfectly even bake.

Problem seven: My baked bread falls apart when I cut it.
Solution: Firstly, it the reason might be you used too much wholewheat flour, as you didn't add enough regular white flour for creating the gluten, which gives it a texture. Not enough water and too much flour can cause crumbly bread. It's a common mistake - people often add more flour if the dough is too sticky rather than kneading through it.

Problem eight: My crust is thin and flimsy.
Solution: A crust is actually pretty tough to achieve at home because it appears from baking in a really good, airtight, hot oven. That's why store-bought factory bread is so crusty - they have such ovens, and they can throw water in to create that blast of steam for a good crust. Some people try to put a tray filled with water at the bottom of the oven, but domestic ovens are mostly not airtight enough to hold that steam in place and let it do something.

Problem nine: My sourdough starter has died.
Solution: These starters die all the time, and it's usually because they've been forgotten about and sat for too long. They have a short shelf life, and they're quite hard to bring back as starters are living creatures with live bacteria. If it's gone pink, moldy, or red, the best thing to do is get rid of it as it's most likely too far gone.

Problem ten: My loaf just cracked during baking.
Solution: When you put the dough in the oven, it expands, but you want to control that. Slightly slashing the loaf horizontally or diagonally cuts through the surface and will encourage it to grow in the specified direction. Using the list above, you can determine what went wrong with your fresh-baked bread and fix that next time. The last advice is: change the ingredients as necessary, make sure you always add what you need, and if you make changes to the recipe, aim to keep the right proportions. That's all there is to it.

Essential Tools for Your Zojirushi Bread Machine
Because your bread maker is so wonderfully self-contained, you won't need a lot of extra equipment to start making amazing bread. Most likely, your bread maker will include things like cooking pans, but you will want to make sure you also have a good-quality cooling rack for your freshly baked bread - placing hot loaves on a flat surface can trap steam on the underside of the bread, leading to a soggy bottom.

And because the one thing your bread maker does not do is slice your bread, you will want to make sure to have a nice, sharp bread knife. Regular knives are usually not serrated and they will have a hard time cleanly cutting the loaf. A bread knife has a wide serrated pattern that allows you to easily saw through the loaf and produce perfectly even slices, no matter what kind of bread you are slicing.

How to Store Your Bread

1. Storing bread dough: Prepare your dough according to the recipe. Allow rising. Then wrap it in a plastic wrap and place it in a plastic container or bag.
- You can refrigerate bread dough for three to four days
- You can freeze bread dough for up to one month

2. Where you slice matters: If you slice your bread at one end, then you will get an open-end moisture "leaking" problem. So slice the loaf in half down the middle, cut servings from the loaves, and then press the loaves back together before storing. This will prevent leaking moisture problems.

3. Wrapping bread in foil or plastic instead of cloth keeps the soft bread longer.

4. If you want to preserve crispy crust, store large crusty loaves on the counter (unwrapped and cut-side down) at room temperature for a day or so.

5. For long-term storage (more than two days), wrap your bread in single-day portions and freeze. Thaw and reheat servings before serving.

6. Breadbox: A large breadbox will give you air circulation and balance humidity to store your bread properly. Do not wrap the bread in paper and then place it in the bread box.

7. Do not refrigerate: Do not keep your homemade bread in the refrigerator because it will stale quickly. However, you can put store-bought bread in the refrigerator.

Bread with added fat such as brioche and challah will take longer to stale. On the other hand, low-fat bread like baguettes will stale quickly.

SPICE, NUT & HERB BREAD

1. Seeded Bread

Servings: 16 Slices
Cooking Time: 40 Minutes
Ingredients:
- Two tablespoons chia seeds
- 1/4 teaspoon salt
- Seven large eggs
- 1/2 teaspoon xanthan gum
- 2 cups almond flour
- One teaspoon baking powder
- 1/2 cup unsalted butter
- Three tablespoons sesame seeds
- Two tablespoons olive oil

Directions:
1. Add all the ingredients to the Bread machine.
2. Close the lid and choose Bread mode. Once done, take out from the machine and cut into at least 16 slices.
3. This seeded bread can be kept for up to 4-5 days in the fridge.

Nutrition Info: Calories: 101 Cal; Fat: 4 g; Cholesterol:; Carbohydrates: 4 g; Protein: 6 g

2. Molasses Candied-ginger Bread

Servings: 1 Loaf
Cooking Time: 10 Minutes
Ingredients:
- 12 slices bread (1½ pounds)
- 1 cup milk, at 80°F to 90°F
- 1 egg, at room temperature
- ¼ cup dark molasses
- 3 tablespoons butter, melted and cooled
- ½ teaspoon salt
- ¼ cup chopped candied ginger
- ½ cup quick oats
- 3 cups white bread flour
- 2 teaspoons bread machine or instant yeast

Directions:
1. Preparing the Ingredients.
2. Choose the size of loaf of your preference and then measure the ingredients.
3. Add all of the ingredients mentioned previously in the list.
4. Close the lid after placing the pan in the bread machine.
5. Select the Bake cycle
6. Turn on the bread machine. Select the White/Basic setting, select the loaf size, and the crust color. Press start.
7. When the cycle is finished, carefully remove the pan from the bread maker and let it rest.
8. Remove the bread from the pan, put in a wire rack to Cool about 5 minutes. Slice

3. Orange Almond Bacon Bread

Servings: 10 Pcs
Cooking Time: 60 Minutes
Ingredients:
- 1 ½ cups almond flour
- One tablespoon baking powder
- 7 oz bacon, diced
- Two eggs
- 1 ½ cups cheddar cheese, shredded
- Four tablespoons butter, melted
- 1/3 cup sour cream

Directions:
1. Add all ingredients to the bread machine.
2. Close the lid and choose the Sweet Bread mode.
3. After the cooking time is over, remove the machine's bread and rest for about 10 minutes.
4. Enjoy!

Nutrition Info: Calories: 307 Cal; Fat: 26 g; Carbohydrate:3 g; Protein: 14 g

4. Garlic, Herb, And Cheese Bread

Servings: One Loaf (12 Slices)
Cooking Time: 15 Minutes
Ingredients:
- 1/2 cup ghee
- Six eggs
- 2 cups almond flour
- 1 tbsp baking powder
- 1/2 tsp xanthan gum
- 1 cup cheddar cheese, shredded
- 1 tbsp garlic powder
- 1 tbsp parsley
- 1/2 tbsp oregano
- 1/2 tsp salt

Directions:
1. Lightly beat eggs and ghee before pouring into bread machine pan.

2. Add the remaining ingredients to the pan.
3. Set bread machine to gluten-free.
4. When the bread is finished, remove the bread pan from the bread machine.
5. Let it cool for a while before transferring into a cooling rack.
6. You can store your bread for up to 5 days in the refrigerator.

Nutrition Info: Calories: 156 ;Carbohydrates: 4g;Protein: 5g;Fat: 13g

5. Italian Pine Nut Bread

Servings: 10
Cooking Time: 3 Hours 30 Minutes
Ingredients:
- Water – 1 cup+ 2 tbsps.
- Bread flour – 3 cups.
- Sugar – 2 tbsps.
- Salt – 1 tsp.
- Active dry yeast – 1 ¼ tsps.
- Basil pesto – 1/3 cup.
- Flour – 2 tbsps.
- Pine nuts – 1/3 cup.

Directions:
1. In a small bowl, mix basil pesto and flour until well blended. Add pine nuts and stir well. Add water, bread flour, sugar, salt, and yeast into the bread machine pan. Select basic setting then select medium crust and press start. Add basil pesto mixture just before the final kneading cycle. Once loaf is done, remove the loaf pan from the machine. Allow it to cool for 10 minutes. Slice and serve.

6. Caramelized Onion Bread

Servings: 14 Slices
Cooking Time: 3 H. 35 Min.
Ingredients:
- ½ Tbsp butter
- ½ cup onions, sliced
- 1 cup water
- 1 Tbsp olive oil
- 3 cups Gold Medal Better for Bread flour
- 2 Tbsp sugar
- 1 tsp salt
- 1¼ tsp bread machine or quick active dry yeast

Directions:
1. Melt the butter over medium-low heat in a skillet.
2. Cook the onions in the butter for 10 to 15 minutes until they are brown and caramelized - then remove from the heat.
3. Add each ingredient except the onions to the bread machine in the order and at the temperature recommended by your bread machine manufacturer.
4. Close the lid, select the basic bread, medium crust setting on your bread machine and press start.
5. Add ½ cup of onions 5 to 10 minutes before the last kneading cycle ends.
6. When the bread machine has finished baking, remove the bread and put it on a cooling rack.

7. Honeyed Bulgur Bread

Servings: 1 Loaf
Cooking Time: 10 Minutes
Ingredients:
- 12 slice bread (1½ pounds)
- ¾ cup boiling water
- 3 tablespoons bulgur wheat
- 3 tablespoons quick oats
- 2 eggs, at room temperature
- 1½ tablespoons melted butter, cooled
- 2¼ tablespoons honey
- 1 teaspoon salt
- 2¼ cups white bread flour
- 1½ teaspoons bread machine or instant yeast

Directions:
1. Preparing the Ingredients.
2. Place the water, bulgur, and oats in the bucket of your bread machine for 30 minutes or until the liquid is 80°F to 90°F.
3. Place the remaining ingredients in your bread machine as recommended by the manufacturer.
4. Select the Bake cycle
5. Turn on the bread machine. Select the White/Basic setting, select the loaf size, and the crust color. Press start.
6. When the cycle is finished, carefully remove the pan from the bread maker and let it rest.
7. Remove the bread from the pan, put in a wire rack to Cool about 5 minutes. Slice

8. Pesto Nut Bread

Servings: 14 Slices
Cooking Time: 10 Minutes
Ingredients:
- 1 cup plus 2 Tbsp water

- 3 cups Gold Medal Better for Bread flour
- 2 Tbsp sugar
- 1 tsp salt
- 1¼ tsp bread machine or quick active dry yeast
- For the pesto filling:
- ⅓ cup basil pesto
- 2 Tbsp Gold Medal Better for Bread flour
- ⅓ cup pine nuts

Directions:
1. Preparing the Ingredients
2. Add each ingredient to the bread machine in the order and at the temperature recommended by your bread machine manufacturer.
3. Select the Bake cycle
4. Close the lid, select the basic bread, medium crust setting on your bread machine, and press start.
5. In a small bowl, combine pesto and 2 Tbsp of flour until well blended. Stir in the pine nuts. Add the filling 5 minutes before the last kneading cycle ends.
6. When the bread machine has finished baking, remove the bread and put it on a cooling rack.

9. French Herb Bread

Servings: 10
Cooking Time: 3 Hours 30 Minutes
Ingredients:
- All-purpose flour – 3 cups
- Instant dry yeast – 2 ½ tsps.
- Sugar – 3 tbsps.
- Garlic powder – ½ tsp.
- Sea salt – 1 ½ tsps.
- Warm water – 1 cup.
- Dried oregano – ½ tsp.
- Dried basil – ½ tsp.
- Dried ground thyme – 1/8 tsp.
- Dried rosemary – 1 tsp.
- Olive oil – 3 tbsps.

Directions:
1. In a small bowl, mix together dried herbs and olive oil and set aside. Add water salt, sugar, yeast, oil herb mixture, and flour into the bread machine pan. Select French bread setting then select light crust and start. Once loaf is done, remove the loaf pan from the machine. Allow it to cool for 10 minutes. Slice and serve.

10. Fragrant Cardamom Bread

Servings: 1 Loaf
Cooking Time: 10 Minutes
Ingredients:
- 12 slices bread (1½ pounds)
- ¾ cup milk, at 80°F to 90°F
- 1 egg, at room temperature
- 1½ teaspoons melted butter, cooled
- 3 tablespoons honey
- 1 teaspoon salt
- 1 teaspoon ground cardamom
- 3 cups white bread flour
- 1¼ teaspoons bread machine or instant yeast

Directions:
1. Preparing the Ingredients.
2. Choose the size of loaf of your preference and then measure the ingredients.
3. Add all of the ingredients mentioned previously in the list.
4. Close the lid after placing the pan in the bread machine.
5. Select the Bake cycle
6. Turn on the bread machine. Select the White/Basic setting, select the loaf size, and the crust color. Press start.
7. When the cycle is finished, carefully remove the pan from the bread maker and let it rest.
8. Remove the bread from the pan, put in a wire rack to Cool about 10 minutes. Slice

11. Tuscan Herb Bread

Servings: 10
Cooking Time: 2 Hours
Ingredients:
- Yeast – 2 tsps.
- Bread flour – 2 1/2 cups
- Italian seasoning – 2 tbsps.
- Sugar – 2 tbsps.
- Olive oil – 2 tbsps.
- Warm water – 1 cup
- Salt – 1 tsp.

Directions:
1. Add olive oil and water to the bread pan. Add remaining ingredients except for yeast to the bread pan. Make a small hole into the flour with your finger and add yeast to the hole. Make sure yeast will not be mixed with any liquids. Select basic setting then select light/medium crust and start.

Once loaf is done, remove the loaf pan from the machine. Allow it to cool for 10 minutes. Slice and serve.

12. Mix Seed Raisin Bread

Servings: 1 Loaf
Cooking Time: 10 Minutes
Ingredients:
- 16 slices bread (2 pounds)
- 1½ cups lukewarm milk
- 2 tablespoons unsalted butter, melted
- 2 tablespoons honey
- 1 teaspoon table salt
- 2½ cups white bread flour
- ¼ cup flaxseed
- ¼ cup sesame seeds
- 1½ cups whole-wheat flour
- 2¼ teaspoons bread machine yeast
- ½ cup raisins

Directions:
1. Preparing the Ingredients.
2. Choose the size of loaf of your preference and then measure the ingredients.
3. Add all of the ingredients mentioned previously in the list.
4. Close the lid after placing the pan in the bread machine.
5. Select the Bake cycle
6. Turn on the bread machine. Select the White/Basic setting, select the loaf size, and the crust color. Press start.
7. When the cycle is finished, carefully remove the pan from the bread maker and let it rest.
8. Remove the bread from the pan, put in a wire rack to Cool about 10 minutes. Slice

13. Garlic Herb Bread

Servings: 8
Cooking Time: 3 Hours And 25 Minutes
Ingredients:
- 1% milk – 1 cup, warm
- Light butter - 1 tbsp.
- White sugar – 1 tbsp.
- Salt – 1 ½ tsp.
- Italian seasoning – 1 ½ tsp.
- Garlic powder – 3 tsp.
- White flour – 3 cups
- Active dry yeast – 2 tsp.

Directions:
1. Add everything according to bread machine recommendations.
2. Select Basic bread cycle and press Start.
3. Remove the bread when done.
4. Cool, slice, and serve.

Nutrition Info: (Per Serving): Calories: 213; Total Fat: 2.8 g; Saturated Fat: 1.4 g; Carbohydrates: 40 g; Cholesterol: 7 mg; Fiber: 1.6 g; Calcium: 46 mg; Sodium: 465 mg; Protein: 6.4 g

14. Cheese Herb Bread

Servings: 10
Cooking Time: 3 Hours 27 Minutes
Ingredients:
- Active dry yeast – 1 ¼ tsps.
- Dried oregano – 1 ¼ tsps.
- Fennel seed – 1 ¼ tsps.
- Dried basil – 1 ¼ tsps.
- Asiago cheese – 2/3 cup, grated
- Bread flour – 3 ¼ cups
- Sugar – 1 tbsp.
- Salt – ¾ tsp.
- Water – 1 cup.

Directions:
1. Add all ingredients to the bread machine. Select sweet bread setting then select light/medium crust and start. Once loaf is done, remove the loaf pan from the machine. Allow it to cool for 10 minutes. Slice and serve.

15. Cardamom Cranberry Bread

Servings: 14 Slices
Cooking Time: 3 H.
Ingredients:
- 1¾ cups water
- 2 Tbsp brown sugar
- 1½ tsp salt
- 2 Tbsp coconut oil
- 4 cups flour
- 2 tsp cinnamon
- 2 tsp cardamom
- 1 cup dried cranberries
- 2 tsp yeast

Directions:
1. Add each ingredient except the dried cranberries to the bread machine in the order and at the temperature recommended by your bread machine manufacturer.

2. Close the lid, select the basic bread, medium crust setting on your bread machine and press start.
3. Add the dried cranberries 5 to 10 minutes before the last kneading cycle ends.
4. When the bread machine has finished baking, remove the bread and put it on a cooling rack.

16. Chocolate Mint Bread

Servings: 1 Loaf
Cooking Time: 10 Minutes
Ingredients:
- 12 slices bread (1½ pounds)
- 1 cup milk, at 80°F to 90°F
- ⅛ teaspoon mint extract
- 1½ tablespoons butter, melted and cooled
- ¼ cup sugar
- 1 teaspoon salt
- 1½ tablespoons unsweetened cocoa powder
- 3 cups white bread flour
- 1¾ teaspoons bread machine or instant yeast
- ½ cup semisweet chocolate chips

Directions:
1. Preparing the Ingredients.
2. Choose the size of loaf of your preference and then measure the ingredients.
3. Add all of the ingredients mentioned previously in the list.
4. Close the lid after placing the pan in the bread machine.
5. Select the Bake cycle
6. Turn on the bread machine. Select the White/Basic setting, select the loaf size, and the crust color. Press start.
7. When the cycle is finished, carefully remove the pan from the bread maker and let it rest.
8. Remove the bread from the pan, put in a wire rack to Cool about 5 minutes. Slice

17. Healthy Basil Whole Wheat Bread

Servings: 10
Cooking Time: 2 Hours
Ingredients:
- Olive oil – 2 tbsps.
- Basil – 1 tbsp.
- Water – 1 1/3 cups
- Whole wheat flour – 4 cups
- Salt – 2 tsps.
- Sugar – 3 tbsps.
- Active dry yeast – 2 tsps.

Directions:
1. Add olive oil and water to the bread pan. Add remaining ingredients except for yeast to the bread pan. Make a small hole into the flour with your finger and add yeast to the hole. Make sure yeast will not be mixed with any liquids. Select whole wheat setting then select light/medium crust and start. Once loaf is done, remove the loaf pan from the machine. Allow it to cool for 5 minutes. Slice and serve.

18. Pumpkin Coconut Almond Bread

Servings: 12 Slices
Cooking Time: 5 Minutes
Ingredients:
- 1/3 cup vegetable oil
- 3 large eggs
- 1 1/2 cups canned pumpkin puree
- 1 cup sugar
- 1 1/2 teaspoons baking powder
- 1/2 teaspoon baking soda
- 1/4 teaspoon salt
- 1 tablespoon allspice
- 3 cups all-purpose flour
- 1/2 cup coconut flakes, plus a small handful for the topping
- 2/3 cup slivered almonds, plus a tablespoonful for the topping
- Non-stick cooking spray

Directions:
1. Preparing the Ingredients
2. Spray bread maker pan with non-stick cooking spray. Mix oil, eggs, and pumpkin in a large mixing bowl.
3. Mix remaining ingredients together in a separate mixing bowl. Add wet ingredients to bread maker pan, and dry ingredients on top.
4. Select the Bake cycle
5. Select Dough cycle and press Start. Open lid and sprinkle top of bread with reserved coconut and almonds.
6. Set to Rapid for 1 hour 30 minutes and bake. Cool for 10 minutes on a wire rack before serving.

19. Sesame French Bread

Servings: 14 Slices

Cooking Time: 3 H. 15 Min.
Ingredients:
- ⅞ cup water
- 1 Tbsp butter, softened
- 3 cups bread flour
- 2 tsp sugar
- 1 tsp salt
- 2 tsp yeast
- 2 Tbsp sesame seeds toasted

Directions:
1. Add each ingredient to the bread machine in the order and at the temperature recommended by your bread machine manufacturer.
2. Close the lid, select the French bread, medium crust setting on your bread machine and press start.
3. When the bread machine has finished baking, remove the bread and put it on a cooling rack.

20. Raisin Seed Bread

Servings: 1 Loaf
Cooking Time: 10 Minutes
Ingredients:
- 12 slice bread (1½ pounds)
- 1 cup plus 2 tablespoons milk, at 80°F to 90°F
- 1½ tablespoons melted butter, cooled
- 1½ tablespoons honey
- ¾ teaspoon salt
- 3 tablespoons flaxseed
- 3 tablespoons sesame seeds
- 1¼ cups whole-wheat flour
- 1¾ cups white bread flour
- 1¾ teaspoons bread machine or instant yeast
- ⅓ cup raisins
-

Directions:
1. Preparing the Ingredients.
2. Choose the size of loaf of your preference and then measure the ingredients.
3. Add all of the ingredients mentioned previously in the list except the raisins.
4. Close the lid after placing the pan in the bread machine.
5. Select the Bake cycle
6. Program the machine for Basic/White bread, select light or medium crust, and press Start.
7. Add the raisins when the bread machine signals, or place the raisins in the raisin/nut hopper and let the machine add them.

8. When the cycle is finished, carefully remove the pan from the bread maker and let it rest.
9. Remove the bread from the pan, put in a wire rack to Cool about 5 minutes. Slice

21. Herb And Garlic Cream Cheese Bread

Servings: 1 Loaf
Cooking Time: 10 Minutes
Ingredients:
- 12 slices bread (1½ pounds)
- ½ cup water, at 80°F to 90°F
- ½ cup herb and garlic cream cheese, at room temperature
- 1 egg, at room temperature
- 2 tablespoons melted butter, cooled
- 3 tablespoons sugar
- 1 teaspoon salt
- 3 cups white bread flour
- 1½ teaspoons bread machine or instant yeast

Directions:
1. Preparing the Ingredients.
2. Choose the size of loaf of your preference and then measure the ingredients.
3. Add all of the ingredients mentioned previously in the list.
4. Close the lid after placing the pan in the bread machine.
5. Select the Bake cycle
6. Turn on the bread machine. Select the White/Basic setting, select the loaf size, and the crust color. Press start.
7. When the cycle is finished, carefully remove the pan from the bread maker and let it rest.
8. Remove the bread from the pan, put in a wire rack to Cool about 10 minutes. Slice

22. Herbed Pesto Bread

Servings: 1 Loaf
Cooking Time: 10 Minutes
Ingredients:
- 12 slices bread (1½ pounds)
- 1 cup water, at 80°F to 90°F
- 2¼ tablespoons melted butter, cooled
- 1½ teaspoons minced garlic
- ¾ tablespoon sugar
- 1 teaspoon salt
- 3 tablespoons chopped fresh parsley
- 1½ tablespoons chopped fresh basil

- ⅓ cup grated Parmesan cheese
- 3 cups white bread flour
- 1¼ teaspoons bread machine or active dry yeast

Directions:
1. Preparing the Ingredients.
2. Choose the size of loaf of your preference and then measure the ingredients.
3. Add all of the ingredients mentioned previously in the list.
4. Close the lid after placing the pan in the bread machine.
5. Select the Bake cycle
6. Turn on the bread machine. Select the White/Basic setting, select the loaf size, and the crust color. Press start.
7. When the cycle is finished, carefully remove the pan from the bread maker and let it rest.
8. Remove the bread from the pan, put in a wire rack to Cool about 10 minutes. Slice

23. Grain, Seed And Nut Bread

Servings: 1 Loaf
Cooking Time: 10 Minutes
Ingredients:
- ¼ cup water
- 1 egg
- 3 Tbsp honey
- 1½ tsp butter, softened
- 3¼ cups bread flour
- 1 cup milk
- 1 tsp salt
- ¼ tsp baking soda
- 1 tsp ground cinnamon
- 2½ tsp active dry yeast
- ¾ cup dried cranberries
- ½ cup chopped walnuts
- 1 Tbsp white vinegar
- ½ tsp sugar

Directions:
1. Preparing the Ingredients.
2. Choose the size of loaf of your preference and then measure the ingredients.
3. Add all of the ingredients mentioned previously in the list.
4. Close the lid after placing the pan in the bread machine.
5. Select the Bake cycle
6. Turn on the bread machine. Select the White/Basic setting, select the loaf size, and the crust color. Press start.
7. When the cycle is finished, carefully remove the pan from the bread maker and let it rest.
8. Remove the bread from the pan, put in a wire rack to Cool about 10 minutes. Slice

24. Rosemary Cranberry Pecan Bread

Servings: 14 Slices
Cooking Time: 3 H.
Ingredients:
- 1⅓ cups water, plus
- 2 Tbsp water
- 2 Tbsp butter
- 2 tsp salt
- 4 cups bread flour
- ¾ cup dried sweetened cranberries
- ¾ cup toasted chopped pecans
- 2 Tbsp non-fat powdered milk
- ¼ cup sugar
- 2 tsp yeast

Directions:
1. Add each ingredient to the bread machine in the order and at the temperature recommended by your bread machine manufacturer.
2. Close the lid, select the basic bread, medium crust setting on your bread machine and press start.
3. When the bread machine has finished baking, remove the bread and put it on a cooling rack.

25. Onion Bacon Bread

Servings: 22 Slices
Cooking Time: 1 Hour
Ingredients:
- 1 ½ cups lukewarm water (80 degrees F)
- Two tablespoons sugar
- Three teaspoons active dry yeast
- 4 ½ cups wheat flour
- One whole egg
- Two teaspoons kosher salt
- One tablespoon olive oil
- Three small onions, chopped and lightly toasted
- 1 cup bacon, chopped

Directions:

1. Prepare all of the ingredients for your bread and measuring means (a cup, a spoon, kitchen scales).
2. Carefully measure the ingredients into the pan, except the bacon and onion.
3. Place all of the ingredients into a bucket in the right order, following the manual for your bread machine.
4. Close the cover.
5. Select the program of your bread machine to BASIC and choose the crust colour to MEDIUM.
6. Press START.
7. After the machine beeps, add the onion and bacon.
8. Wait until the program completes.
9. When done, take the bucket out and let it cool for 5-10 minutes.
10. Shake the loaf from the pan and let cool for 30 minutes on a cooling rack.
11. Slice, serve and enjoy the taste of fragrant Homemade Bread.

Nutrition Info: Calories: 391 Cal;Fat: 9.7 g;Cholesterol: 38 g;Sodium: 960 mg;Carbohydrates: 59.9 g;Total Sugars 1.2g;Protein 3.4g;Potassium 43mg

26. Basic Pecan Bread

Servings: 1 Loaf

Ingredients:
- 16 slice bread (2 pounds)
- 1⅓ cups lukewarm milk
- 2⅔ tablespoons unsalted butter, melted
- 1 egg, at room temperature
- 2⅔ tablespoons sugar
- 1⅓ teaspoons table salt
- 4 cups white bread flour
- 2 teaspoons bread machine yeast
- 1⅓ cups chopped pecans, toasted
- 12 slice bread (1½ pounds)
- 1 cup lukewarm milk
- 2 tablespoons unsalted butter, melted
- 1 egg, at room temperature
- 2 tablespoons sugar
- 1 teaspoon table salt
- 3 cups white bread flour
- 1½ teaspoons bread machine yeast
- 1 cup chopped pecans, toasted

Directions:

1. Choose the size of loaf you would like to make and measure your ingredients.
2. Add all of the ingredients except for the toasted pecans to the bread pan in the order listed above.
3. Place the pan in the bread machine and close the lid.
4. Turn on the bread maker. Select the White/Basic or Fruit/Nut (if your machine has this setting) setting, then the loaf size, and finally the crust color. Start the cycle.
5. When the machine signals to add ingredients, add the toasted pecans. (Some machines have a fruit/nut hopper where you can add the toasted pecans when you start the machine. The machine will automatically add them to the dough during the baking process.)
6. When the cycle is finished and the bread is baked, carefully remove the pan from the machine. Use a potholder as the handle will be very hot. Let rest for a few minutes.
7. Remove the bread from the pan and allow to cool on a wire rack for at least 10 minutes before slicing.

Nutrition Info: (Per Serving):Calories 168, fat 4.8 g, carbs 25.6 g, sodium 217 mg, protein 5 g

27. Delicious Cranberry Bread

Servings: 10
Cooking Time: 3 Hours 27 Minutes

Ingredients:
- Warm water – 1 ½ cups
- Brown sugar – 2 tbsps.
- Salt – 1 ½ tsps.
- Olive oil – 2 tbsps.
- Flour – 4 cups
- Cinnamon – 1 ½ tsps.
- Cardamom – 1 ½ tsps.
- Dried cranberries – 1 cup
- Yeast – 2 tsps.

Directions:

1. Add all ingredients to the bread machine in the listed order. Select sweet bread setting then select light/medium crust and start. Once loaf is done, remove the loaf pan from the machine. Allow it to cool for 20 minutes. Slice and serve.

28. Market Seed Bread

Servings: 1 Loaf

Cooking Time: 10 Minutes
Ingredients:
- 12 slice bread (1½ pounds)
- 1 cup plus 2 tablespoons milk, at 80°F to 90°F
- 1½ tablespoons melted butter, cooled
- 1½ tablespoons honey
- ¾ teaspoon salt
- 3 tablespoons flaxseed
- 3 tablespoons sesame seeds
- 1½ tablespoons poppy seeds
- 1¼ cups whole-wheat flour
- 1¾ cups white bread flour
- 1¾ teaspoons bread machine or instant yeast

Directions:
1. Preparing the Ingredients.
2. Choose the size of loaf of your preference and then measure the ingredients.
3. Add all of the ingredients mentioned previously in the list.
4. Close the lid after placing the pan in the bread machine.
5. Select the Bake cycle
6. Turn on the bread machine. Select the White/Basic setting, select the loaf size, and the crust color. Press start.
7. When the cycle is finished, carefully remove the pan from the bread maker and let it rest.
8. Remove the bread from the pan, put in a wire rack to Cool about 5 minutes. Slice

29. Pistachio Cherry Bread

Servings: 1 Loaf
Ingredients:
- 16 slice bread (2 pounds)
- 1⅛ cups lukewarm water
- 1 egg, at room temperature
- ¼ cup butter, softened
- ¼ cup packed dark brown sugar
- 1½ teaspoons table salt
- 3¾ cups white bread flour
- ½ teaspoon ground nutmeg
- Dash allspice
- 2 teaspoons bread machine yeast
- 1 cup dried cherries
- ½ cup unsalted pistachios, chopped
- 12 slice bread (1½ pounds)
- ¾ cup lukewarm water
- 1 egg, at room temperature
- 3 tablespoons butter, softened
- 3 tablespoons packed dark brown sugar
- 1⅛ teaspoons table salt
- 2¾ cups white bread flour
- ½ teaspoon ground nutmeg
- Dash allspice
- 1½ teaspoons bread machine yeast
- ¾ cup dried cherries
- ⅓ cup unsalted pistachios, chopped

Directions:
1. Choose the size of loaf you would like to make and measure your ingredients.
2. Add all of the ingredients except for the pistachios and cherries to the bread pan in the order listed above.
3. Place the pan in the bread machine and close the lid.
4. Turn on the bread maker. Select the White/Basic or Fruit/Nut (if your machine has this setting) setting, then the loaf size, and finally the crust color. Start the cycle.
5. When the machine signals to add ingredients, add the pistachios and cherries. (Some machines have a fruit/nut hopper where you can add the pistachios and cherries when you start the machine. The machine will automatically add them to the dough during the baking process.)
6. When the cycle is finished and the bread is baked, carefully remove the pan from the machine. Use a potholder as the handle will be very hot. Let rest for a few minutes.
7. Remove the bread from the pan and allow to cool on a wire rack for at least 10 minutes before slicing.

Nutrition Info: (Per Serving):Calories 196, fat 5.3 g, carbs 27.8 g, sodium 237 mg, protein 4.4 g

30. Cinnamon Bread

Servings: 1 Loaf
Cooking Time: 10 Minutes
Ingredients:
- 12 slices bread (1½ pounds)
- 1 cup milk, at 80°F to 90°F
- 1 egg, at room temperature
- ¼ cup melted butter, cooled
- ½ cup sugar
- ½ teaspoon salt
- 1½ teaspoons ground cinnamon
- 3 cups white bread flour

- 2 teaspoons bread machine or active dry yeast

Directions:
1. Preparing the Ingredients.
2. Choose the size of loaf of your preference and then measure the ingredients.
3. Add all of the ingredients mentioned previously in the list.
4. Close the lid after placing the pan in the bread machine.
5. Select the Bake cycle
6. Turn on the bread machine. Select the White/Basic setting, select the loaf size, and the crust color. Press start.
7. When the cycle is finished, carefully remove the pan from the bread maker and let it rest.
8. Remove the bread from the pan, put in a wire rack to Cool about 10 minutes. Slice

31. Oatmeal Seed Bread

Servings: 1 Loaf
Cooking Time: 10 Minutes
Ingredients:
- 12 slice bread (1½ pounds)
- 1⅛ cups water, at 80°F to 90°F
- 3 tablespoons melted butter, cooled
- 3 tablespoons light brown sugar
- 1½ teaspoons salt
- 3 tablespoons raw sunflower seeds
- 3 tablespoons pumpkin seeds
- 2 tablespoons sesame seeds
- 1 teaspoon anise seeds
- 1 cup quick oats
- 2¼ cups white bread flour
- 1½ teaspoons bread machine or instant yeast

Directions:
1. Preparing the Ingredients.
2. Choose the size of loaf of your preference and then measure the ingredients.
3. Add all of the ingredients mentioned previously in the list.
4. Close the lid after placing the pan in the bread machine.
5. Select the Bake cycle
6. Turn on the bread machine. Select the White/Basic setting, select the loaf size, and the crust color. Press start.
7. When the cycle is finished, carefully remove the pan from the bread maker and let it rest.

8. Remove the bread from the pan, put in a wire rack to Cool about 5 minutes. Slice

32. Seed Bread

Servings: 1 Loaf
Cooking Time: 10 Minutes
Ingredients:
- 3 Tbsp flax seed
- 1 Tbsp sesame seeds
- 1 Tbsp poppy seeds
- ¾ cup water
- 1 Tbsp honey
- 1 Tbsp canola oil
- ½ tsp salt
- 1½ cups bread flour
- 5 Tbsp wholemeal flour
- 1¼ tsp dried active baking yeast

Directions:
1. Preparing the Ingredients
2. Add each ingredient to the bread machine in the order and at the temperature recommended by your bread machine manufacturer.
3. Select the Bake cycle
4. Close the lid, select the basic bread, medium crust setting on your bread machine, and press start.
5. When the bread machine has finished baking, remove the bread and put it on a cooling rack.

33. Coffee Raisin Bread

Servings: 10
Cooking Time: 3 Hours
Ingredients:
- Active dry yeast – 2 ½ tsps.
- Ground cloves – ¼ tsp.
- Ground allspice – ¼ tsp.
- Ground cinnamon – 1 tsp.
- Sugar – 3 tbsps.
- Egg – 1, lightly beaten
- Olive oil – 3 tbsps.
- Strong brewed coffee – 1 cup.
- Bread flour – 3 cups.
- Raisins – ¾ cup.
- Salt – 1 ½ tsps.

Directions:
1. Add all ingredients except for raisins into the bread machine pan. Select basic setting then select light/medium crust and press start. Add raisins just before the final kneading cycle. Once loaf is done,

remove the loaf pan from the machine. Allow it to cool for 10 minutes. Slice and serve.

34. Almond Milk Bread

Servings: 1 Loaf
Ingredients:
- 16 slice bread (2 pounds)
- 1 cup lukewarm milk
- 2 eggs, at room temperature
- 2⅔ tablespoons butter, melted and cooled
- ⅓ cup sugar
- 1 teaspoon table salt
- 2⅓ teaspoons lemon zest
- 4 cups white bread flour
- 2¼ teaspoons bread machine yeast
- ½ cup slivered almonds, chopped
- ½ cup golden raisins, chopped
- 12 slice bread (1½ pounds)
- ¾ cup lukewarm milk
- 2 eggs, at room temperature
- 2 tablespoons butter, melted and cooled
- ¼ cup sugar
- 1 teaspoon table salt
- 2 teaspoons lemon zest
- 3 cups white bread flour
- 2 teaspoons bread machine yeast
- ⅓ cup slivered almonds, chopped
- ⅓ cup golden raisins, chopped

Directions:
1. Choose the size of loaf you would like to make and measure your ingredients.
2. Add all of the ingredients except for the raisins and almonds to the bread pan in the order listed above.
3. Place the pan in the bread machine and close the lid.
4. Turn on the bread maker. Select the White/Basic or Fruit/Nut (if your machine has this setting) setting, then the loaf size, and finally the crust color. Start the cycle.
5. When the machine signals to add ingredients, add the raisins and almonds. (Some machines have a fruit/nut hopper where you can add the raisins and almonds when you start the machine. The machine will automatically add them to the dough during the baking process.)
6. When the cycle is finished and the bread is baked, carefully remove the pan from the machine. Use a potholder as the handle will be very hot. Let rest for a few minutes.
7. Remove the bread from the pan and allow to cool on a wire rack for at least 10 minutes before slicing.

Nutrition Info: (Per Serving):Calories 193, fat 4.6 g, carbs 29.4 g, sodium 214 mg, protein 5.7 g

35. Lavender Buttermilk Bread

Servings: 14 Slices
Cooking Time: 3 H.
Ingredients:
- ½ cup water
- ⅞ cup buttermilk
- ¼ cup olive oil
- 3 Tbsp finely chopped fresh lavender leaves
- 1 ¼ tsp finely chopped fresh lavender flowers
- Grated zest of 1 lemon
- 4 cups bread flour
- 2 tsp salt
- 2 ¾ tsp bread machine yeast

Directions:
1. Add each ingredient to the bread machine in the order and at the temperature recommended by your bread machine manufacturer.
2. Close the lid, select the basic bread, medium crust setting on your bread machine and press start.
3. When the bread machine has finished baking, remove the bread and put it on a cooling rack.

36. Olive Bread

Servings: 14 Slices
Cooking Time: 3 H.
Ingredients:
- ½ cup brine from olive jar
- Add warm water (110°F) To make 1½ cup when combined with brine
- 2 Tbsp olive oil
- 3 cups bread flour
- 1⅔ cups whole wheat flour
- 1½ tsp salt
- 2 Tbsp sugar
- 1½ tsp dried leaf basil
- 2 tsp active dry yeast
- ⅔ cup finely chopped Kalamata olives

Directions:
1. Add each ingredient except the olives to the bread machine in the order and at the temperature

recommended by your bread machine manufacturer.
2. Close the lid, select the wheat, medium crust setting on your bread machine and press start.
3. Add the olives 10 minutes before the last kneading cycle ends.
4. When the bread machine has finished baking, remove the bread and put it on a cooling rack.

37. Spicy Cajun Bread

Servings: 1 Loaf
Cooking Time: 10 Minutes
Ingredients:
- 12 slice bread (1½ pounds)
- 1⅛ cups water, at 80°F to 90°F
- 1½ tablespoons melted butter, cooled
- 1 tablespoon tomato paste
- 1½ tablespoons sugar
- 1½ teaspoons salt
- 3 tablespoons skim milk powder
- ¾ tablespoon Cajun seasoning
- ¼ teaspoon onion powder
- 3 cups white bread flour
- 1¼ teaspoons bread machine or instant yeast

Directions:
1. Preparing the Ingredients.
2. Choose the size of loaf of your preference and then measure the ingredients.
3. Add all of the ingredients mentioned previously in the list.
4. Close the lid after placing the pan in the bread machine.
5. Select the Bake cycle
6. Turn on the bread machine. Select the White/Basic setting, select the loaf size, and the crust color. Press start.
7. When the cycle is finished, carefully remove the pan from the bread maker and let it rest.
8. Remove the bread from the pan, put in a wire rack to Cool about 10 minutes. Slice

38. Pumpkin Cinnamon Bread

Servings: 14 Slices
Cooking Time: 3 H.
Ingredients:
- 1 cup sugar
- 1 cup canned pumpkin
- ⅓ cup vegetable oil
- 1 tsp vanilla
- 2 eggs
- 1½ cups all-purpose bread flour
- 2 tsp baking powder
- ¼ tsp salt
- 1 tsp ground cinnamon
- ¼ tsp ground nutmeg
- ⅛ tsp ground cloves

Directions:
1. Add each ingredient to the bread machine in the order and at the temperature recommended by your bread machine manufacturer.
2. Close the lid, select the quick, medium crust setting on your bread machine and press start.
3. When the bread machine has finished baking, remove the bread and put it on a cooling rack.

39. Cajun Bread

Servings: 14 Slices
Cooking Time: 10 Minutes
Ingredients:
- ½ cup water
- ¼ cup chopped onion
- ¼ cup chopped green bell pepper
- 2 tsp finely chopped garlic
- 2 tsp soft butter
- 2 cups bread flour
- 1 Tbsp sugar
- 1 tsp Cajun
- ½ tsp salt
- 1 tsp active dry yeast

Directions:
1. Preparing the Ingredients
2. Add each ingredient to the bread machine in the order and at the temperature recommended by your bread machine manufacturer.
3. Select the Bake cycle
4. Close the lid, select the basic bread, medium crust setting on your bread machine and press start.
5. When the bread machine has finished baking, remove the bread and put it on a cooling rack.

40. Aromatic Lavender Bread

Servings: 1 Loaf
Cooking Time: 10 Minutes
Ingredients:
- 16 slices bread (2 pounds)
- 1½ cups milk, at 80°F to 90°F
- 2 tablespoons melted butter, cooled
- 2 tablespoons sugar

- 2 teaspoons salt
- 2 teaspoons chopped fresh lavender flowers
- 1 teaspoon lemon zest
- ½ teaspoon chopped fresh thyme
- 4 cups white bread flour
- 1½ teaspoons bread machine or instant yeast

Directions:
1. Preparing the Ingredients.
2. Choose the size of loaf of your preference and then measure the ingredients.
3. Add all of the ingredients mentioned previously in the list.
4. Close the lid after placing the pan in the bread machine.
5. Select the Bake cycle
6. Turn on the bread machine. Select the White/Basic setting, select the loaf size, and the crust color. Press start.
7. When the cycle is finished, carefully remove the pan from the bread maker and let it rest.
8. Remove the bread from the pan, put in a wire rack to Cool about 10 minutes. Slice

41. Cracked Black Pepper Bread

Servings: 1 Loaf
Cooking Time: 10 Minutes
Ingredients:
- 12 slice bread (1½ pounds)
- 1⅛ cups water, at 80°F to 90°F
- 1½ tablespoons melted butter, cooled
- 1½ tablespoons sugar
- 1 teaspoon salt
- 3 tablespoons skim milk powder
- 1½ tablespoons minced chives
- ¾ teaspoon garlic powder
- ¾ teaspoon freshly cracked black pepper
- 3 cups white bread flour
- 1¼ teaspoons bread machine or instant yeast

Directions:
1. Preparing the Ingredients.
2. Choose the size of loaf of your preference and then measure the ingredients.
3. Add all of the ingredients mentioned previously in the list.
4. Close the lid after placing the pan in the bread machine.
5. Select the Bake cycle
6. Turn on the bread machine. Select the White/Basic setting, select the loaf size, and the crust color. Press start.
7. When the cycle is finished, carefully remove the pan from the bread maker and let it rest.
8. Remove the bread from the pan, put in a wire rack to Cool about 10 minutes. Slice

42. Whole-wheat Seed Bread

Servings: 1 Loaf
Cooking Time: 10 Minutes
Ingredients:
- 12 slice bread (1½ pounds)
- 1⅛ cups water, at 80°F to 90°F
- 1½ tablespoons honey
- 1½ tablespoons melted butter, cooled
- ¾ teaspoon salt
- 2½ cups whole-wheat flour
- ¾ cup white bread flour
- 3 tablespoons raw sunflower seeds
- 1 tablespoon sesame seeds
- 1½ teaspoons bread machine or instant yeast

Directions:
1. Preparing the Ingredients.
2. Choose the size of loaf of your preference and then measure the ingredients.
3. Add all of the ingredients mentioned previously in the list.
4. Close the lid after placing the pan in the bread machine.
5. Select the Bake cycle
6. Turn on the bread machine. Select the Whole-Wheat/Whole-Grain bread, select the loaf size, and select light or medium crust. Press start.
7. When the cycle is finished, carefully remove the pan from the bread maker and let it rest.
8. Remove the bread from the pan, put in a wire rack to Cool about 5 minutes. Slice

43. Semolina Bread

Servings: 6 Pcs
Cooking Time: One Hour
Ingredients:
- Almond fine flour, one cup
- Semolina flour, one cup
- Yeast, one teaspoon
- An egg
- Salt, one teaspoon
- Stevia powder, two teaspoons

- Olive oil extra virgin, two teaspoons
- Water warm, one cup
- Sesame seeds, two teaspoons

Directions:
1. Get a mixing container and combine the almond flour, semolina flour, salt, and stevia powder.
2. In another mixing container, combine the egg
3. extra virgin olive oil, and warm water.
4. By instructions on your machine's manual, pour the ingredients in the bread pan and follow how to mix in the yeast.
5. Put the bread pan in the machine, select the basic bread setting
6. together with the bread size and crust type, if available, then press start once you have closed the machine's lid.
7. When the bread is ready, open the lid and spread the sesame seeds at the top and close for a few minutes.
8. By using oven mitts, remove the pan from the machine. Use a stainless spatula to extract the pan's bread and turn the pan upside down on a metallic rack where the bread will cool off before slicing it.

Nutrition Info: Calories: 100;Carbohydrates: 2.8g;Protein: 5g;Fat: 14g

44. Whole Wheat Raisin Bread

Servings: 10
Cooking Time: 2 Hours
Ingredients:
- Whole wheat flour – 3 ½ cups
- Dry yeast – 2 tsps.
- Eggs – 2, lightly beaten
- Butter – ¼ cup, softened
- Water – ¾ cup
- Milk – 1/3 cup
- Salt – 1 tsp.
- Sugar – 1/3 cup
- Cinnamon – 4 tsps.
- Raisins – 1 cup

Directions:
1. Add water, milk, butter, and eggs to the bread pan. Add remaining ingredients except for yeast to the bread pan. Make a small hole into the flour with your finger and add yeast to the hole. Make sure yeast will not be mixed with any liquids. Select whole wheat setting then select light/medium crust

and start. Once loaf is done, remove the loaf pan from the machine. Allow it to cool for 10 minutes. Slice and serve.

45. Pumpkin Pie Spice Bread

Servings: 12
Cooking Time: 1 Hour And 20 Minutes
Ingredients:
- Brown sugar – ½ cup
- White sugar – ½ cup
- Canned pumpkin – 1 cup
- Oil – 1/3 cup
- Vanilla – 1 tsp.
- Eggs – 2
- All-purpose flour – 1 ½ cups
- Baking powder – 2 tsp.
- Salt – ¼ tsp.
- Pumpkin pie spice – 1 ½ tsp.
- Chopped walnuts – ½ cup

Directions:
1. Add everything according to bread machine recommendation.
2. Select Quick bread cycle and Medium crust. Press Start.
3. Remove the bread when done.
4. Cool, slice, and serve.

Nutrition Info: (Per Serving): Calories: 225; Total Fat: 10 g; Saturated Fat: 1 g; Carbohydrates: 31 g; Cholesterol: 31 mg; Fiber: 1 g; Calcium: 25 mg; Sodium: 145 mg; Protein: 4 g

46. Oatmeal Sunflower Bread

Servings: 10
Cooking Time: 3 Hours 30 Minutes
Ingredients:
- Water – 1 cup.
- Honey – ¼ cup.
- Butter – 2 tbsps., softened
- Bread flour – 3 cups.
- Old fashioned oats – ½ cup.
- Milk powder – 2 tbsps.
- Salt – 1 ¼ tsps.
- Active dry yeast – 2 ¼ tsps.
- Sunflower seeds – ½ cup.

Directions:
1. Add all ingredients except for sunflower seeds into the bread machine pan. Select basic setting then select light/medium crust and press start. Add sunflower seeds just before the final kneading cycle.

Once loaf is done, remove the loaf pan from the machine. Allow it to cool for 10 minutes. Slice and serve.

47. Fragrant Herb Bread

Servings: 1 Loaf
Cooking Time: 10 Minutes
Ingredients:
- 12 slices bread (1½ pounds)
- 1⅛ cups water, at 80°F to 90°F
- 1½ tablespoons melted butter, cooled
- 1½ tablespoons sugar
- 1 teaspoon salt
- 3 tablespoons skim milk powder
- 1 teaspoon dried thyme
- 1 teaspoon dried chives
- 1 teaspoon dried oregano
- 3 cups white bread flour
- 1¼ teaspoons bread machine or instant yeast

Directions:
1. Preparing the Ingredients.
2. Choose the size of loaf of your preference and then measure the ingredients.
3. Add all of the ingredients mentioned previously in the list. Close the lid after placing the pan in the bread machine.
4. Select the Bake cycle
5. Turn on the bread machine. Select the White/Basic setting, select the loaf size, and the crust color. Press start.
6. When the cycle is finished, carefully remove the pan from the bread maker and let it rest.
7. Remove the bread from the pan, put in a wire rack to Cool about 10 minutes. Slice

48. Anise Lemon Bread

Servings: 1 Loaf
Cooking Time: 10 Minutes
Ingredients:
- 12 slice bread (1½ pounds)
- ¾ cup water, at 80°F to 90°F
- 1 egg, at room temperature
- ¼ cup butter, melted and cooled
- ¼ cup honey
- ½ teaspoon salt
- 1 teaspoon anise seed
- 1 teaspoon lemon zest
- 3 cups white bread flour
- 2 teaspoons bread machine or instant yeast

Directions:
1. Preparing the Ingredients.
2. Choose the size of loaf of your preference and then measure the ingredients.
3. Add all of the ingredients mentioned previously in the list.
4. Close the lid after placing the pan in the bread machine.
5. Select the Bake cycle
6. Turn on the bread machine. Select the White/Basic setting, select the loaf size, and the crust color. Press start.
7. When the cycle is finished, carefully remove the pan from the bread maker and let it rest.
8. Remove the bread from the pan, put in a wire rack to Cool about 10 minutes. Slice

49. Macadamia Bread

Servings: 8 Pcs
Cooking Time: 60 Minutes
Ingredients:
- ¼ cup almond flour
- 1 cup macadamia nuts
- Two tablespoons flax meal
- One teaspoon baking powder
- Two scoops of whey protein powder
- Four eggs
- Two egg whites
- One tablespoon lemon juice
- ¼ cup butter, melted

Directions:
1. Add all the ingredients to the Bread machine.
2. Close the lid and choose Express Bake mode. Once done, take out from the machine and cut into at least 16 slices.

Nutrition Info: Calories: 257 Cal;Fat: 22.4g ;Carbohydrates: 4.5g ;Protein: 11.5g

50. Dilly Onion Bread

Servings: 14 Slices
Cooking Time: 3 H. 5 Min.
Ingredients:
- ¾ cup water (70°F to 80°F)
- 1 Tbsp butter, softened
- 2 Tbsp sugar
- 3 Tbsp dried minced onion
- 2 Tbsp dried parsley flakes
- 1 Tbsp dill weed
- 1 tsp salt

- 1 garlic clove, minced
- 2 cups bread flour
- ⅓ cup whole wheat flour
- 1 Tbsp nonfat dry milk powder
- 2 tsp active dry yeast serving

Directions:
1. Add each ingredient to the bread machine in the order and at the temperature recommended by your bread machine manufacturer.
2. Close the lid, select the basic bread, medium crust setting on your bread machine and press start.
3. When the bread machine has finished baking, remove the bread and put it on a cooling rack.

51. Turmeric Bread

Servings: 14 Slices
Cooking Time: 3 H.
Ingredients:

- 1 tsp dried yeast
- 4 cups strong white flour
- 1 tsp turmeric powder
- 2 tsp beetroot powder
- 2 Tbsp olive oil
- 1.5 tsp salt
- 1 tsp chili flakes
- 1⅜ water

Directions:
1. Add each ingredient to the bread machine in the order and at the temperature recommended by your bread machine manufacturer.
2. Close the lid, select the basic bread, medium crust setting on your bread machine and press start.
3. When the bread machine has finished baking, remove the bread and put it on a cooling rack.

FRUIT AND VEGETABLE BREAD

52. Fruit Raisin Bread

Servings: 14 Slices
Cooking Time: 3 H. 5 Min.
Ingredients:
- 1 egg
- 1 cup water plus 2 Tbsp
- ½ tsp ground cardamom.
- 1 tsp salt
- 1½ Tbsp sugar
- ¼ cup butter, softened
- 3 cups bread flour
- 1 tsp bread machine yeast
- ⅓ cup raisins
- ⅓ cup mixed candied fruit

Directions:
1. Add each ingredient except the raisins and fruitcake mix to the bread machine in the order and at the temperature recommended by your bread machine manufacturer.
2. Close the lid, select the basic bread, medium crust setting on your bread machine, and press start.
3. Add raisins and fruit at the fruit/nut beep or 5 to 10 minutes before the last kneading cycle ends.
4. When the bread machine has finished baking, remove the bread and put it on a cooling rack.

53. Fresh Blueberry Bread

Servings: 1 Loaf
Cooking Time: 10 Minutes
Ingredients:
- 12 to 16 slices (1½ to 2 pounds)
- 1 cup plain Greek yogurt, at room temperature
- ½ cup milk, at room temperature
- 3 tablespoons butter, at room temperature
- 2 eggs, at room temperature
- ½ cup sugar
- ¼ cup light brown sugar
- 1 teaspoon pure vanilla extract
- ½ teaspoon lemon zest
- 2 cups all-purpose flour
- 1 tablespoon baking powder
- ¾ teaspoon salt
- ¼ teaspoon ground nutmeg
- 1 cup blueberries

Directions:
1. Preparing the Ingredients.
2. Place the yogurt, milk, butter, eggs, sugar, brown sugar, vanilla, and zest in your bread machine.
3. Select the Bake cycle.
4. Program the machine for Quick/Rapid bread and press Start. While the wet ingredients are mixing, stir together the flour, baking powder, salt, and nutmeg in a medium bowl. After the first fast mixing is done and the machine signals, add the dry ingredients. When the second mixing cycle is complete, stir in the blueberries. When the loaf is done, remove the bucket from the machine. Let the loaf cool for 5 minutes. Gently shake the bucket to remove the loaf, and turn it out onto a rack to cool.

54. Garlic Olive Bread

Servings: 1 Loaf
Cooking Time: 10 Minutes
Ingredients:
- 12 slice bread (1½ pounds)
- 1 cup lukewarm milk
- 1½ tablespoons unsalted butter, melted
- 1 teaspoon garlic, minced
- 1½ tablespoons sugar
- 1 teaspoon table salt
- 3 cups white bread flour
- 1 teaspoon bread machine yeast
- ⅓ cup black olives, chopped
- 16 slice bread (2 pounds)
- 1⅓ cups lukewarm milk
- 2 tablespoons unsalted butter, melted
- 1⅓ teaspoons garlic, minced
- 2 tablespoons sugar
- 1⅓ teaspoons table salt
- 4 cups white bread flour
- 1½ teaspoons bread machine yeast
- ½ cup black olives, chopped

Directions:
1. Preparing the Ingredients
2. Choose the size of loaf of your preference and then measure the ingredients.
3. Add all of the ingredients mentioned previously in the list, except for the olives. Close the lid after placing the pan in the bread machine.
4. Select the Bake

5. Turn on the bread machine. White/Basic or Fruit/Nut (if your machine has this setting) setting, select the loaf size, and the crust color. Press start.
6. When the machine signals to add ingredients, add the olives. When the cycle is finished, carefully remove the pan from the bread maker and let it rest.
7. Remove the bread from the pan, put in a wire rack to cool for at least 10 minutes, and slice.

55. Garlic Onion Pepper Bread

Servings: 10
Cooking Time: 2 Hours
Ingredients:
- Water – ½ cup.
- Onion – ¼ cup., chopped
- Bell pepper – ¼ cup., chopped
- Garlic – 2 tsps., chopped
- Butter – 2 tsps.
- Bread flour – 2 cups.
- Sugar – 1 tbsp.
- Cajun seasoning – 1 tsp.
- Salt – ½ tsp.
- Active dry yeast – 1 tsp.

Directions:
1. Add all ingredients into the bread machine pan. Select basic bread setting then select medium crust and press start. Once loaf is done, remove the loaf pan from the machine. Allow it to cool for 10 minutes. Slice and serve.

56. Honey Banana Bread

Servings: 1 Loaf
Ingredients:
- 16 slice bread (2 pounds)
- ⅔ cup lukewarm milk
- 1⅓ cups banana, mashed
- 1 egg, beaten
- 2 tablespoons unsalted butter, melted
- ¼ cup honey
- 1⅓ teaspoons pure vanilla extract
- ⅔ teaspoon table salt
- 1⅓ cups whole-wheat flour
- 1⅔ cups white bread flour
- 2 teaspoons bread machine yeast
- 12 slice bread (1½ pounds)
- ½ cup lukewarm milk
- 1 cup banana, mashed
- 1 egg, beaten
- 1½ tablespoons unsalted butter, melted
- 3 tablespoons honey
- 1 teaspoon pure vanilla extract
- ½ teaspoon table salt
- 1 cup whole-wheat flour
- 1¼ cups white bread flour
- 1½ teaspoons bread machine yeast

Directions:
1. Choose the size of loaf you would like to make and measure your ingredients.
2. Add the ingredients to the bread pan in the order listed above.
3. Place the pan in the bread machine and close the lid.
4. Turn on the bread maker. Select the Sweet setting, then the loaf size, and finally the crust color. Start the cycle.
5. When the cycle is finished and the bread is baked, carefully remove the pan from the machine. Use a potholder as the handle will be very hot. Let rest for a few minutes.
6. Remove the bread from the pan and allow to cool on a wire rack for at least 10 minutes before slicing.

Nutrition Info: (Per Serving):Calories 153, fat 3.4 g, carbs 27.1 g, sodium 131 mg, protein 4.2 g

57. Spice Peach Bread

Servings: 1 Loaf
Ingredients:
- 16 slice bread (2 pounds)
- ½ cup lukewarm heavy whipping cream
- 1 egg, beaten
- 1½ tablespoons unsalted butter, melted
- 3 tablespoons sugar
- 1½ teaspoons table salt
- ¼ teaspoon nutmeg, ground
- ½ teaspoon cinnamon, ground
- 3½ cups white bread flour
- ½ cup whole-wheat flour
- 1½ teaspoons bread machine yeast
- 1 cup canned peaches, drained and chopped
- 12 slice bread (1½ pounds)
- ⅓ cup lukewarm heavy whipping cream
- 1 egg, beaten
- 1 tablespoon unsalted butter, melted
- 2¼ tablespoons sugar
- 1⅛ teaspoons table salt

- ⅛ teaspoon nutmeg, ground
- ⅓ teaspoon cinnamon, ground
- 2⅔ cups white bread flour
- ⅓ cup whole-wheat flour
- 1⅛ teaspoons bread machine yeast
- ¾ cup canned peaches, drained and chopped

Directions:
1. Choose the size of loaf you would like to make and measure your ingredients.
2. Add all of the ingredients except for the peach to the bread pan in the order listed above.
3. Place the pan in the bread machine and close the lid.
4. Turn on the bread maker. Select the White/Basic or Fruit/Nut (if your machine has this setting) setting, then the loaf size, and finally the crust color. Start the machine.
5. When the machine signals to add ingredients, add the peaches. (Some machines have a fruit/nut hopper where you can add the peaches when you start the machine. The machine will automatically add them to the dough during the baking process.)
6. When the cycle is finished and the bread is baked, carefully remove the pan from the machine. Use a potholder as the handle will be very hot. Let rest for a few minutes.
7. Remove the bread from the pan and allow to cool on a wire rack for at least 10 minutes before slicing.

Nutrition Info: (Per Serving):Calories 157, fat 3.1 g, carbs 26.4 g, sodium 197 mg, protein 4.2 g

58. Blueberry-basil Loaf

Servings: 1 Loaf
Cooking Time: 10 Minutes
Ingredients:
- 12 slice bread (1½ pounds)
- 1¼ cups fresh blueberries
- 1 tablespoon all-purpose flour
- 2¼ cups all-purpose flour
- 1 cup granulated sugar
- 2 teaspoons baking powder
- 1 teaspoon grated lemon peel
- ½ teaspoon salt
- 1 cup buttermilk
- 6 tablespoons butter, melted
- 1 teaspoon vanilla
- 2 eggs
- ¼ cup coarsely chopped fresh basil leaves
- Topping
- ½ cup packed brown sugar
- ¼ cup butter, melted
- ⅔ cup all-purpose flour

Directions:
1. Preparing the Ingredients.
2. Choose the size of loaf of your preference and then measure the ingredients.
3. Add all of the ingredients mentioned previously in the list. Close the lid after placing the pan in the bread machine.
4. Select the Bake cycle
5. Turn on the bread machine. Select the White/Basic setting, select the loaf size, and the crust color. Press start.
6. When the cycle is finished, carefully remove the pan from the bread maker and let it rest.
7. Remove the bread from the pan, put in a wire rack to Cool about 1 hour.

59. Cranberry & Golden Raisin Bread

Servings: 14 Slices
Cooking Time: 10 Minutes
Ingredients:
- 1⅓ cups water
- 4 Tbsp sliced butter
- 3 cups flour
- 1 cup old fashioned oatmeal
- ⅓ cup brown sugar
- 1 tsp salt
- 4 Tbsp dried cranberries
- 4 Tbsp golden raisins
- 2 tsp bread machine yeast

Directions:
1. Preparing the Ingredients
2. Add each ingredient except cranberries and golden raisins to the bread machine one by one, according to the manufacturer's instructions.
3. Select the Bake cycle
4. Close the lid, select the sweet or basic bread, medium crust setting on your bread machine and press start.
5. Add the cranberries and golden raisins 5 to 10 minutes before the last kneading cycle ends.
6. When the bread machine has finished baking, remove the bread and put it on a cooling rack.

60. Gluten-free Cinnamon Raisin Bread

Servings: 12 Slices
Cooking Time: 5 Minutes
Ingredients:
- 3/4 cup almond milk
- 2 tablespoons flax meal
- 6 tablespoons warm water
- 1 1/2 teaspoons apple cider vinegar
- 2 tablespoons butter
- 1 1/2 tablespoons honey
- 1 2/3 cups brown rice flour
- 1/4 cup corn starch
- 2 tablespoons potato starch
- 1 1/2 teaspoons xanthan gum
- 1 tablespoon cinnamon
- 1/2 teaspoon salt
- 1 teaspoon active dry yeast
- 1/2 cup raisins

Directions:
1. Preparing the Ingredients.
2. Mix together flax and water and let stand for 5 minutes.
3. Combine dry ingredients in a separate bowl, except for yeast.
4. Add wet ingredients to the bread machine.
5. Add the dry mixture on top and make a well in the middle of the dry mixture.
6. Add the yeast to the well.
7. Select the Bake cycle
8. Set to Gluten Free, light crust color, and press Start. After first kneading and rise cycle, add raisins.
9. Remove to a cooling rack when baked and let cool for 15 minutes before slicing.

61. Strawberry Oat Bread

Servings: 1 Loaf
Cooking Time: 10 Minutes
Ingredients:
- 16 slice bread (2 pounds)
- 1½ cups lukewarm milk
- ¼ cup unsalted butter, melted
- ¼ cup sugar
- 2 teaspoons table salt
- 1½ cups quick oats
- 3 cups white bread flour
- 2 teaspoons bread machine yeast
- 1 cup strawberries, sliced

Directions:
1. Preparing the Ingredients.
2. Choose the size of loaf of your preference and then measure the ingredients.
3. Add all of the ingredients mentioned previously in the list, except for the strawberries. Close the lid after placing the pan in the bread machine.
4. Select the Bake cycle
5. Turn on the bread machine. White/Basic or Fruit/Nut (if your machine has this setting) setting, select the loaf size, and the crust color. Press start.
6. When the machine signals to add ingredients, add the strawberries. When the cycle is finished, carefully remove the pan from the bread maker and let it rest.
7. Remove the bread from the pan, put in a wire rack to cool for at least 10 minutes, and slice.

62. Chocolate-pistachio Bread

Servings: 2/3 Cup (24 Slices)
Cooking Time: 10 Minutes
Ingredients:
- 2/3 cup granulated sugar
- ½ cup butter, melted
- ¾ cup milk
- 1 egg
- 1½ cups all-purpose flour
- 1 cup chopped pistachio nuts
- ½ cup semisweet chocolate chips
- 1/3 cup unsweetened baking cocoa
- 2 teaspoons baking powder
- ¼ teaspoon salt
- Decorator sugar crystals, if desired

Directions:
1. Preparing the Ingredients.
2. Choose the size of loaf of your preference and then measure the ingredients.
3. Add all of the ingredients mentioned previously in the list. Close the lid after placing the pan in the bread machine.
4. Select the Bake cycle
5. Turn on the bread machine. Select the White/Basic setting, select the loaf size, and the crust color. Press start.
6. When the cycle is finished, carefully remove the pan from the bread maker and let it rest.

7. Remove the bread from the pan, put in a wire rack to cool for at least 2 hours. Wrap tightly and store at room temperature up to 4 days, or refrigerate.

63. Blueberry Bread

Servings: 10
Cooking Time: 2 Hours
Ingredients:
- Milk – ¾ cup.
- Egg – 1
- Water – 3 tbsps.
- Butter – 2 tbsps.
- Sugar – 3 tbsps.
- Salt – ¾ tsp.
- Ground nutmeg – ¼ tsp.
- Dried blueberries – 1/3 cup.
- Bread flour – 3 cups.
- Active dry yeast – 1 tsp.

Directions:
1. Add all ingredients into the bread machine pan. Select basic setting then select medium crust and start. Once loaf is done, remove the loaf pan from the machine. Allow it to cool for 10 minutes. Slice and serve.

64. Oatmeal-streusel Bread

Servings: 1 Loaf
Cooking Time: 10 Minutes
Ingredients:
- Streusel
- ¼ cup packed brown sugar
- ¼ cup chopped walnuts, toasted
- 2 teaspoons ground cinnamon
- Bread
- 1 cup all-purpose flour
- ½ cup whole wheat flour
- ½ cup old-fashioned oats
- 2 tablespoons ground flaxseed or flaxseed meal
- 1 teaspoon baking powder
- ½ teaspoon salt
- ¼ teaspoon baking soda
- ¾ cup packed brown sugar
- 2/3 cup vegetable oil
- 2 eggs
- ¼ cup sour cream
- 2 teaspoons vanilla
- ½ cup milk
- Icing
- ¾ to 1 cup powdered sugar
- 1 tablespoon milk
- 2 teaspoons light corn syrup

Directions:
1. Preparing the Ingredients.
2. Choose the size of loaf of your preference and then measure the ingredients.
3. Add all of the ingredients mentioned previously in the list. Close the lid after placing the pan in the bread machine
4. Select the Bake cycle.
5. Turn on the bread machine. Select the White/Basic setting, select the loaf size, and the crust color. Press start.
6. When the cycle is finished, carefully remove the pan from the bread maker and let it rest.
7. Remove the bread from the pan, put in a wire rack to Cool completely, about 2 hours.
8. In small bowl, beat all icing ingredients, adding enough of the powdered sugar for desired drizzling consistency. Drizzle icing over bread. Let stand until set. Wrap tightly and store at room temperature up to 4 days, or refrigerate. To toast walnuts, bake in ungreased shallow pan at 350°F for 7 to 11 minutes, stirring occasionally, until light brown.

65. Mushroom Leek Bread

Servings: 10
Cooking Time: 2 Hours
Ingredients:
- Butter – 2 tbsps.
- Mushrooms – 2 cups., sliced
- Leeks – ¾ cup., sliced
- Dried thyme – 1 ½ tsps.
- Water – 1 1/3 cup.
- Salt – 1 ½ tsps.
- Honey – 2 tbsps.
- Whole wheat flour – 1 ¼ cups.
- Bread flour – 3 cups.
- Yeast – 1 tsp.

Directions:
1. Heat butter into the saucepan over medium-high heat. Add leeks, mushrooms, and thyme and sauté until tender. Transfer mushroom leek mixture into the bread machine pan. Add remaining ingredients into the bread machine pan. Select basic setting then select medium crust and

start. Once loaf is done, remove the loaf pan from the machine. Allow it to cool for 10 minutes. Slice and serve.

66.   Poppy Seed–lemon Bread

Servings: 1 Loaf
Cooking Time: 10 Minutes
Ingredients:
- 1 cup sugar
- ¼ cup grated lemon peel
- 1 cup milk
- ¾ cup vegetable oil
- 2 tablespoons poppy seed
- 2 teaspoons baking powder
- ½ teaspoon salt
- 2 eggs, slightly beaten

Directions:
1. Preparing the Ingredients.
2. Choose the size of loaf of your preference and then measure the ingredients.
3. Add all of the ingredients mentioned previously in the list. Close the lid after placing the pan in the bread machine
4. Select the Bake cycle
5. Turn on the bread machine. Select the White/Basic setting, select the loaf size, and the crust color. Press start.
6. When the cycle is finished, carefully remove the pan from the bread maker and let it rest.
7. Remove the bread from the pan, put in a wire rack to cool completely, about 2 hours. Wrap tightly and store at room temperature up to 4 days, or refrigerate.

67.   Beetroot Bread

Servings: 1 Loaf
Ingredients:
- 16 slice bread (2 pounds)
- 1 cup lukewarm water
- 1 cup grated raw beetroot
- 2 tablespoons unsalted butter, melted
- 2 tablespoons sugar
- 2 teaspoons table salt
- 4 cups white bread flour
- 1⅔ teaspoons bread machine yeast
- 12 slice bread (1½ pounds)
- ¾ cups lukewarm water
- ¾ cup grated raw beetroot
- 1½ tablespoons unsalted butter, melted
- 1½ tablespoons sugar
- 1¼ teaspoons table salt
- 3 cups white bread flour
- 1¼ teaspoons bread machine yeast

Directions:
1. Choose the size of loaf you would like to make and measure your ingredients.
2. Add the ingredients to the bread pan in the order listed above.
3. Place the pan in the bread machine and close the lid.
4. Turn on the bread maker. Select the White/Basic setting, then the loaf size, and finally the crust color. Start the cycle.
5. When the cycle is finished and the bread is baked, carefully remove the pan from the machine. Use a potholder as the handle will be very hot. Let rest for a few minutes.
6. Remove the bread from the pan and allow to cool on a wire rack for at least 10 minutes before slicing.

Nutrition Info: (Per Serving):Calories 143, fat 2.3 g, carbs 26.4 g, sodium 268 mg, protein 4 g

68.   Onion Chive Bread

Servings: 1 Loaf
Ingredients:
- 16 slice bread (2 pounds)
- 1¼ cups lukewarm water
- ¼ cup unsalted butter, melted
- 2 tablespoons sugar
- 1½ teaspoons table salt
- 4¼ cups white bread flour
- ¼ cup dried minced onion
- 2 tablespoons fresh chives, chopped
- 2¼ teaspoons bread machine yeast
- 12 slice bread (1½ pounds)
- 1 cup lukewarm water
- 3 tablespoons unsalted butter, melted
- 1½ tablespoons sugar
- 1⅛ teaspoons table salt
- 3⅛ cups white bread flour
- 3 tablespoons dried minced onion
- 1½ tablespoons fresh chives, chopped
- 1⅔ teaspoons bread machine yeast

Directions:
1. Choose the size of loaf you would like to make and measure your ingredients.

2. Add the ingredients to the bread pan in the order listed above.
3. Place the pan in the bread machine and close the lid.
4. Turn on the bread maker. Select the White/Basic setting, then the loaf size, and finally the crust color. Start the cycle.
5. When the cycle is finished and the bread is baked, carefully remove the pan from the machine. Use a potholder as the handle will be very hot. Let rest for a few minutes.
6. Remove the bread from the pan and allow to cool on a wire rack for at least 10 minutes before slicing.

Nutrition Info: (Per Serving):Calories 147, fat 3 g, carbs 26.2 g, sodium 223 mg, protein 4.6 g

69. Basil Tomato Bread

Servings: 14 Slices
Cooking Time: 10 Minutes
Ingredients:
- 2¼ tsp dried active baking yeast
- 1⅝ cups bread flour
- 3 Tbsp wheat bran
- 5 Tbsp quinoa
- 3 Tbsp dried milk powder
- 1 Tbsp dried basil
- 25g sun-dried tomatoes, chopped
- 1 tsp salt
- 1⅛ cups water
- 1 cup boiling water to cover tomatoes

Directions:
1. Preparing the Ingredients.
2. Cover dried tomatoes with boiling water in a bowl.
3. Soak for 10 minutes, drain, and cool to room temperature.
4. Snip tomatoes into small pieces, using scissors.
5. Add each ingredient to the bread machine in the order and at the temperature recommended by your bread machine manufacturer.
6. Select the Bake cycle
7. Close the lid, select the basic bread, medium crust setting on your bread machine and press start.
8. When the bread machine has finished baking, remove the bread and put it on a cooling rack.

70. Apple-fig Bread With Honey Glaze

Servings: 1 Loaf
Cooking Time: 10 Minutes
Ingredients:
- 1½ cups all-purpose flour
- 1½ teaspoons ground cinnamon
- 1 teaspoon baking powder
- ½ teaspoon salt
- ½ teaspoon ground nutmeg
- ¼ teaspoon ground allspice
- ⅔ cup granulated sugar
- ½ cup vegetable oil
- 1 egg
- 1 egg yolk
- 1½ teaspoons vanilla
- ½ cup milk
- 1 cup chopped peeled apples
- ½ cup dried figs, chopped glaze
- ⅓ to ½ cup powdered sugar
- 2 tablespoons honey
- 1 tablespoon butter, softened
- Dash ground allspice

Directions:
1. Preparing the Ingredients.
2. Choose the size of loaf of your preference and then measure the ingredients.
3. Add all of the ingredients mentioned previously in the list. Close the lid after placing the pan in the bread machine
4. Select the Bake cycle
5. Turn on the bread machine. Select the White/Basic setting, select the loaf size, and the crust color. Press start.
6. When the cycle is finished, carefully remove the pan from the bread maker and let it rest.
7. Remove the bread from the pan, put in a wire rack to cool. Cool completely, about 2 hours. In small bowl, beat ⅓ cup powdered sugar, the honey, butter and dash of allspice until smooth, slowly adding additional powdered sugar for desired glaze consistency. Spread glaze over top of loaf. Let stand until set. (Glaze will remain slightly tacky to the touch.) Wrap tightly and store in refrigerator.

71. Plum Orange Bread

Servings: 1 Loaf
Cooking Time: 10 Minutes

Ingredients:
- 12 slice bread (1½ pounds)
- 1⅛ cup water, at 80°F to 90°F
- 2¼ tablespoons melted butter, cooled
- 3 tablespoons sugar
- ¾ teaspoon salt
- ¾ teaspoon orange zest
- ⅓ teaspoon ground cinnamon
- Pinch ground nutmeg
- 1¾ cups plus 2 tablespoons whole-wheat flour
- 1⅛ cups white bread flour
- 1½ teaspoons bread machine or instant yeast
- 1 cup chopped fresh plums

Directions:
1. Preparing the Ingredients.
2. Choose the size of loaf of your preference and then measure the ingredients.
3. Add all of the ingredients mentioned previously in the list, except for the plums. Close the lid after placing the pan in the bread machine.
4. Select the Bake cycle
5. Turn on the bread machine. White/Basic or Fruit/Nut (if your machine has this setting) setting, select the loaf size, and the crust color. Press start.
6. When the machine signals to add ingredients, add the plums. When the cycle is finished, carefully remove the pan from the bread maker and let it rest.
7. Remove the bread from the pan, put in a wire rack to cool for at least 10 minutes, and slice.

72. Blueberries 'n Orange Bread

Servings: 1 Loaf
Cooking Time: 10 Minutes
Ingredients:
- 18 slices bread
- 3 cups Original Bisquick mix
- ½ cup granulated sugar
- 1 tablespoon grated orange peel
- ½ cup milk
- 3 tablespoons vegetable oil
- 2 eggs
- 1 cup fresh or frozen (rinsed and drained) blueberries glaze
- ½ cup powdered sugar
- 3 to 4 teaspoons orange juice
- Additional grated orange peel, if desired

Directions:
1. Preparing the Ingredients.
2. Choose the size of loaf of your preference and then measure the ingredients.
3. Add all of the ingredients mentioned previously in the list. Close the lid after placing the pan in the bread machine.
4. Select the Bake cycle
5. Program the machine for Basic/White bread, select light or medium crust, and press Start. When the loaf is done, remove the bucket from the machine. Let the loaf cool for 5 minutes.
6. Gently shake the bucket to remove the loaf, and turn it out onto a rack to cool. Cool completely, about 45 minutes.
7. In small bowl, mix powdered sugar and orange juice until smooth and thin enough to drizzle. Drizzle glaze over bread; sprinkle with additional orange peel.

73. Cranberry Honey Bread

Servings: 1 Loaf
Ingredients:
- 16 slice bread (2 pounds)
- 1¼ cups + 1 tablespoon lukewarm water
- ¼ cup unsalted butter, melted
- 3 tablespoons honey or molasses
- 4 cups white bread flour
- ½ cup cornmeal
- 2 teaspoons table salt
- 2½ teaspoons bread machine yeast
- ¾ cup cranberries, dried
- 12 slice bread (1½ pounds)
- 1 cup + 1 tablespoon lukewarm water
- 2 tablespoons unsalted butter, melted
- 3 tablespoons honey or molasses
- 3 cups white bread flour
- ⅓ cup cornmeal
- 1½ teaspoons table salt
- 2 teaspoons bread machine yeast
- ½ cup cranberries, dried

Directions:
1. Choose the size of loaf you would like to make and measure your ingredients.
2. Add all of the ingredients except for the dried cranberries to the bread pan in the order listed above.
3. Place the pan in the bread machine and close the lid.
4. Turn on the bread maker. Select the White/Basic or Fruit/Nut (if your machine has this

setting) setting, then the loaf size, and finally the crust color. Start the cycle.
5. When the machine signals to add ingredients, add the dried cranberries. (Some machines have a fruit/nut hopper where you can add the dried cranberries when you start the machine. The machine will automatically add them to the dough during the baking process.)
6. When the cycle is finished and the bread is baked, carefully remove the pan from the machine. Use a potholder as the handle will be very hot. Let rest for a few minutes.
7. Remove the bread from the pan and allow to cool on a wire rack for at least 10 minutes before slicing.
Nutrition Info: (Per Serving):Calories 174, fat 2.6 g, carbs 33.6 g, sodium 310 mg, protein 4 g

74. Raisin Candied Fruit Bread

Servings: 1 Loaf
Cooking Time: 10 Minutes
Ingredients:
- 16 slice bread (2 pounds)
- 1 egg, beaten
- 1½ cups + 1 tablespoon lukewarm water
- ⅔ teaspoon ground cardamom
- 1¼ teaspoons table salt
- 2 tablespoons sugar
- ⅓ cup butter, melted
- 4 cups bread flour
- 1¼ teaspoons bread machine yeast
- ½ cup raisins
- ½ cup mixed candied fruit

Directions:
1. Preparing the Ingredients.
2. Choose the size of loaf of your preference and then measure the ingredients.
3. Add all of the ingredients mentioned previously in the list, except for the candied fruits and raisins. Close the lid after placing the pan in the bread machine.
4. Select the Bake cycle
5. Turn on the bread machine. White/Basic or Fruit/Nut (if your machine has this setting) setting, select the loaf size, and the crust color. Press start.
6. When the machine signals to add ingredients, add the candied fruits and raisins. When the cycle is finished, carefully remove the pan from the bread maker and let it rest.

7. Remove the bread from the pan, put in a wire rack to cool for at least 10 minutes, and slice.

75. Gluten-free Glazed Lemon-pecan Bread

Servings: 1 Loaf
Cooking Time: 10 Minutes
Ingredients:
- 12 slice bread (1½ pounds)
- ½ cup white rice flour
- ½ cup tapioca flour
- ½ cup potato starch
- ¼ cup sweet white sorghum flour
- ¼ cup garbanzo and fava flour
- 1 teaspoon xanthan gum
- 1 teaspoon gluten-free baking powder
- 1 teaspoon baking soda
- ½ teaspoon salt
- 2 eggs
- ½ cup sunflower or canola oil or melted ghee
- ¼ cup almond milk, soymilk or regular milk
- ½ teaspoon cider vinegar
- 1 tablespoon grated lemon peel
- ¼ cup fresh lemon juice
- ⅔ cup granulated sugar
- ½ cup chopped pecans
- glaze
- 2 tablespoons fresh lemon juice
- 1 cup gluten-free powdered sugar

Directions:
1. Preparing the Ingredients.
2. Choose the size of loaf of your preference and then measure the ingredients.
3. Add all of the ingredients mentioned previously in the list. Close the lid after placing the pan in the bread machine.
4. Select the Bake cycle.
5. Turn on the bread machine. Select the White/Basic setting, select the loaf size, and the crust color. Press start. When the cycle is finished, carefully remove the pan from the bread maker and let it rest.
6. Remove the bread from the pan, put in a wire rack to Cool about 10 minutes.
7. In small bowl, stir all glaze ingredients until smooth. With fork, poke holes in top of loaf; drizzle glaze over loaf. Serve warm.

76. Squash Carrot Bread

Servings: 8 Pcs
Cooking Time: 1 Hour And 30 Minutes
Ingredients:
- One small zucchini
- One baby carrot
- 1 cup whey
- 1 ½ cups (180 g) white wheat flour
- ¾ cup (100 g) whole wheat flour
- ¾ cup (100 g) rye flour
- Two tablespoons vegetable oil
- One teaspoon yeast, fresh
- One teaspoon salt
- ½ teaspoon sugar

Directions:
1. Cut/dice carrots and zucchini to about 8-10 mm (1/2 inch) in size.
2. In a frying pan, heat the vegetable oil, then fry the vegetables over medium heat until soft. If desired, season the vegetables with salt and pepper.
3. Transfer the vegetables to a flat plate so that they cool down more quickly. While still hot, they cannot be added to the dough.
4. Now dissolve the yeast in the serum.
5. Send all kinds of flour, serum with yeast, as well as salt and sugar to the bakery.
6. Knead the dough in the dough for the Rolls program.
7. At the very end of the batch, add the vegetables to the dough.
8. After adding vegetables, the dough will become moister at the end of the fermentation, which will last about an hour before doubling the dough's volume, shift it onto a thickly floured surface.
9. Form into a loaf and put it in an oiled form.
10. Cover the form with a food film and leave for 1 to 1 1/3 hours.
11. Preheat oven to 450°F and put bread in it.
12. Bake the bread for 15 minutes, and then gently remove it from the mould. Lay it on the grate and bake for 15-20 minutes more

Nutrition Info: Calories 220;Total Fat 4.3g;Saturated Fat 0.8g;Cholesterol 0g;Sodium 313mg;Total Carbohydrate 39.1g;Dietary Fiber 4.1g;Total Sugars 2.7g;Protein 6.6g

77. Monkey Bread

Servings: 12 - 15
Cooking Time: 2 Hours
Ingredients:
- 1 cup water
- 1 cup butter, unsalted
- 2 tablespoons butter, softened
- 3 cups all-purpose flour
- 1 teaspoon ground cinnamon
- 1 teaspoon salt
- 1/4 cup white sugar
- 2 1/2 teaspoons active dry yeast
- 1 cup brown sugar, packed
- 1 cup raisins
- Flour, for surface

Directions:
1. Add ingredients, except 1 cup butter, brown sugar, raisins and yeast, to bread maker pan in order listed above.
2. Make a well in the center of the dry ingredients and add the yeast. Make sure that no liquid comes in contact with the yeast.
3. Select Dough cycle and press Start.
4. Place finished dough on floured surface and knead 10 times.
5. Melt one cup of butter in small saucepan.
6. Stir in brown sugar and raisins and mix until smooth. Remove from heat.
7. Cut dough into one inch chunks.
8. Drop one chunk at a time into the butter sugar mixture. Thoroughly coat dough pieces, then layer them loosely in a greased Bundt pan.
9. Let rise in a warm, draft-free space; about 15 to 20 minutes.
10. Bake at 375°F for 20 to 25 minutes or until golden brown.
11. Remove from oven, plate, and serve warm.

Nutrition Info: Calories: 294, Sodium: 265. Mg, Dietary Fiber: 1.3 g, Fat: 14.1 g, Carbs: 40 g, Protein: 3.3 g.

78. Brown Sugar Date Nut Swirl Bread

Servings: 16
Cooking Time: 2 Hours 30 Minutes
Ingredients:
- 1 cup milk
- 1 large egg
- 4 tablespoons butter
- 4 tablespoons sugar
- 1 teaspoon salt
- 4 cups flour

- 1 2/3 teaspoons yeast
- For the filling:
- 1/2 cup packed brown sugar
- 1 cup walnuts, chopped
- 1 cup medjool dates, pitted and chopped
- 2 teaspoons cinnamon
- 2 teaspoons clove spice
- 1 1/3 tablespoons butter
- Powdered sugar, sifted

Directions:
1. Add wet ingredients to the bread maker pan.
2. Mix flour, sugar and salt and add to pan.
3. Make a well in the center of the dry ingredients and add the yeast.
4. Select the Dough cycle and press Start.
5. Punch the dough down and allow it to rest in a warm place.
6. Mix the brown sugar with walnuts, dates and spices; set aside.
7. Roll the dough into a rectangle, on a lightly floured surface.
8. Baste with a tablespoon of butter, add the filling.
9. Start from the short side and roll the dough to form a jelly roll shape.
10. Place the roll into a greased loaf pan and cover.
11. Let it rise in a warm place, until nearly doubled in size; about 30 minutes.
12. Bake at 350°F for approximately 30 minutes.
13. Cover with foil during the last 10 minutes of cooking.
14. Transfer to a cooling rack for 15 minutes; sprinkle with the powdered sugar and serve.

Nutrition Info: Calories: 227, Sodium: 197 mg, Dietary Fiber: 1.5 g, Fat: 8.3 g, Carbs: 33.1 g, Protein: 5.5 g.

79. Zucchini Spice Bread

Servings: 1 Loaf
Ingredients:
- 16 slice bread (2 pounds)
- 2 eggs, at room temperature
- ⅔ cup unsalted butter, melted
- ⅔ teaspoon table salt
- 1 cup shredded zucchini
- ⅔ cup light brown sugar
- 3 tablespoons sugar
- 2 cups all-purpose flour
- ⅔ teaspoon baking powder
- ⅔ teaspoon baking soda
- ⅓ teaspoon ground allspice
- 1⅓ teaspoons ground cinnamon
- ⅔ cup chopped pecans
- 12 slice bread (1½ pounds)
- 2 eggs, at room temperature
- ½ cup unsalted butter, melted
- ½ teaspoon table salt
- ¾ cup shredded zucchini
- ½ cup light brown sugar
- 2 tablespoons sugar
- 1½ cups all-purpose flour
- ½ teaspoon baking powder
- ½ teaspoon baking soda
- ¼ teaspoon ground allspice
- 1 teaspoon ground cinnamon
- ½ cup chopped pecans

Directions:
1. Choose the size of loaf you would like to make and measure your ingredients.
2. Add the ingredients to the bread pan in the order listed above.
3. Place the pan in the bread machine and close the lid.
4. Turn on the bread maker. Select the Quick/Rapid setting, then the loaf size, and finally the crust color. Start the cycle.
5. When the cycle is finished and the bread is baked, carefully remove the pan from the machine. Use a potholder as the handle will be very hot. Let rest for a few minutes.
6. Remove the bread from the pan and allow to cool down on a wire rack for at least 10 minutes or more before slicing.

Nutrition Info: (Per Serving):Calories 167, fat 8.3 g, carbs 19.7 g, sodium 223 mg, protein 3.2 g

80. Perfect Sweet Potato Bread

Servings: 10
Cooking Time: 3 Hours
Ingredients:
- Sweet potato – 1, mashed
- Milk powder – 2 tbsps.
- Salt – 1 ½ tsps.
- Brown sugar – 1/3 cup.
- Butter – 2 tbsps., softened
- Cinnamon – ½ tsp.
- Bread flour – 4 cups.

- Vanilla extract – 1 tsp.
- Warm water – ½ cup.

Directions:
1. Add water, vanilla, bread flour, cinnamon, butter, brown sugar, salt, yeast, milk powder, and sweet potato into the bread machine pan. Select white bread setting then select light crust and press start. Once loaf is done, remove the loaf pan from the machine. Allow it to cool for 10 minutes. Slice and serve.

81. Confetti Bread

Servings: 1 Loaf
Cooking Time: 10 Minutes
Ingredients:
- 8 slice bread (1 pounds)
- ⅓ cup milk, at 80°F to 90°F
- 2 tablespoons water, at 80°F to 90°F
- 2 teaspoons melted butter, cooled
- ⅔ teaspoon white vinegar
- 4 teaspoons sugar
- ⅔ teaspoon salt
- 4 teaspoons grated Parmesan cheese
- ⅓ cup quick oats
- 1⅔ cups white bread flour
- 1 teaspoon bread machine or instant yeast
- ⅓ cup finely chopped zucchini
- ¼ cup finely chopped yellow bell pepper
- ¼ cup finely chopped red bell pepper
- 4 teaspoons chopped chives

Directions:
1. Preparing the Ingredients.
2. Place the ingredients, except the vegetables, in your bread machine as recommended by the manufacturer.
3. Select the Bake cycle
4. Program the machine for Basic/White bread, select light or medium crust, and press Start.
5. When the machine signals, add the chopped vegetables; if your machine has no signal, add the vegetables just before the second kneading is finished.
6. When the cycle is finished, carefully remove the pan from the bread maker and let it rest.
7. Remove the bread from the pan, put in a wire rack to Cool about 10 minutes. Slice

82. Savory Onion Bread

Servings: 1 Loaf
Cooking Time: 10 Minutes
Ingredients:
- 12 slice bread (1½ pounds)
- 1 cup water, at 80°F to 90°F
- 3 tablespoons melted butter, cooled
- 1½ tablespoons sugar
- 1⅛ teaspoons salt
- 3 tablespoons dried minced onion
- 1½ tablespoons chopped fresh chives
- 3 cups plus 2 tablespoons white bread flour
- 1⅔ teaspoons bread machine or instant yeast

Directions:
1. Preparing the Ingredients.
2. Place the ingredients in your bread machine as recommended by the manufacturer.
3. Select the Bake cycle
4. Turn on the bread machine. Select the White/Basic setting, select the loaf size, and the crust color. Press start.
5. When the cycle is finished, carefully remove the pan from the bread maker and let it rest.
6. Remove the bread from the pan, put in a wire rack to Cool about 5 minutes. Slice

83. Black Olive Bread

Servings: 1 Loaf
Cooking Time: 10 Minutes
Ingredients:
- 12 slices (1½ pounds)
- 1 cup milk, at 80°F to 90°F
- 1½ tablespoons melted butter, cooled
- 1 teaspoon minced garlic
- 1½ tablespoons sugar
- 1 teaspoon salt
- 3 cups white bread flour
- 1 teaspoon bread machine or instant yeast
- ⅓ cup chopped black olives

Directions:
1. Preparing the Ingredients.
2. Choose the size of loaf of your preference and then measure the ingredients.
3. Add all of the ingredients mentioned previously in the list. Close the lid after placing the pan in the bread machine.
4. Select the Bake cycle
5. Turn on the bread machine. Select the White/Basic setting, select the loaf size, and the crust color. Press start.

6. When the cycle is finished, carefully remove the pan from the bread maker and let it rest.
7. Remove the bread from the pan, put in a wire rack to cool for at least 10 minutes.

84. Yeasted Carrot Bread

Servings: 1 Loaf
Cooking Time: 10 Minutes
Ingredients:
- 12 slice bread (1½ pounds)
- ¾ cup milk, at 80°F to 90°F
- 3 tablespoons melted butter, cooled
- 1 tablespoon honey
- 1½ cups shredded carrot
- ¾ teaspoon ground nutmeg
- ½ teaspoon salt
- 3 cups white bread flour
- 2¼ teaspoons bread machine or active dry yeast

Directions:
1. Preparing the Ingredients.
2. Choose the size of loaf of your preference and then measure the ingredients.
3. Add all of the ingredients mentioned previously in the list.
4. Close the lid after placing the pan in the bread machine.
5. Select the Bake cycle
6. Turn on the bread machine. Select the Quick/Rapid setting, select the loaf size, and the crust color. Press start.
7. When the cycle is finished, carefully remove the pan from the bread maker and let it rest.
8. Remove the bread from the pan, put in a wire rack to Cool about 5 minutes. Slice

85. Ginger-topped Pumpkin Bread

Servings: 2 Loaves (24 Slices Each)
Cooking Time: 10 Minutes
Ingredients:
- 1 can (15 oz) pumpkin (not pumpkin pie mix)
- 1⅔ cups granulated sugar
- ⅔ cup unsweetened applesauce
- ½ cup milk
- 2 teaspoons vanilla
- 1 cup fat-free egg product or 2 eggs plus 4 egg whites 3 cups all-purpose flour
- 2 teaspoons baking soda
- 1 teaspoon salt
- 1 teaspoon ground cinnamon
- ½ teaspoon baking powder
- ½ teaspoon ground cloves
- glaze and topping
- ⅔ cup powdered sugar
- 2 to 3 teaspoons warm water
- ¼ teaspoon vanilla
- 3 tablespoons finely chopped crystallized ginger

Directions:
1. Preparing the Ingredients.
2. Choose the size of loaf of your preference and then measure the ingredients.
3. Add all of the ingredients mentioned previously in the list. Close the lid after placing the pan in the bread machine.
4. Select the Bake cycle
5. Turn on the bread machine. Select the White/Basic setting, select the loaf size, and the crust color. Press start.
6. When the cycle is finished, carefully remove the pan from the bread maker and let it rest.
7. Remove the bread from the pan, put in a wire rack to cool for at least 2 hours. In small bowl, mix powdered sugar, water and ¼ teaspoon vanilla until thin enough to drizzle. Drizzle over loaves. Sprinkle with ginger. Wrap tightly and store at room temperature up to 4 days, or refrigerate up to 10 days.

86. Delicious Apple Bread

Servings: 10
Cooking Time: 3 Hours 27 Minutes
Ingredients:
- Buttermilk – 1 cup.
- Apple juice concentrate – ¼ cup.
- Butter – 1 ½ tbsps.
- Brown sugar – 3 tbsps.
- Ground cinnamon – 1 ½ tsp.
- Apples – 1 cup., peeled and chopped
- Salt – 1 tsp.
- Bread flour – 3 ½ cups.
- Vital wheat gluten – 4 tsps.
- Yeast – 2 tsps.

Directions:
1. Add all ingredients to the bread machine as listed order. Select sweet bread setting then select light/medium crust and start. Once loaf is done,

remove the loaf pan from the machine. Allow it to cool for 15 minutes. Slice and serve.

87. Zucchini Bread

Servings: 2 Loaves
Cooking Time: 10 Minutes
Ingredients:
- 3 cups shredded zucchini (2 to 3 medium)
- 1⅔ cups sugar
- ⅔ cup vegetable oil
- 2 teaspoons vanilla
- 4 eggs
- 3 cups all-purpose or whole wheat flour
- 2 teaspoons baking soda
- 1 teaspoon salt
- 1 teaspoon ground cinnamon
- ½ teaspoon baking powder
- ½ teaspoon ground cloves
- ½ cup chopped nuts
- ½ cup raisins, if desired

Directions:
1. Preparing the Ingredients.
2. Choose the size of loaf of your preference and then measure the ingredients.
3. Add all of the ingredients mentioned previously in the list. Close the lid after placing the pan in the bread machine.
4. Select the Bake cycle
5. Turn on the bread machine. Select the White/Basic setting, select the loaf size, and the crust color. Press start.
6. When the cycle is finished, carefully remove the pan from the bread maker and let it rest.
7. Remove the bread from the pan, put in a wire rack to cool for at least 2 hours before slicing. Wrap tightly and store at room temperature up to 4 days, or refrigerate up to 10 days.

88. Olive Rosemary Bread

Servings: 10
Cooking Time: 3 Hours 27 Minutes
Ingredients:
- Water – 1 cup.
- Olives – 1 cup., pitted and quartered
- Salt – 1 tsp.
- Sugar – 1 tbsp.
- Olive oil – 2 tbsps.
- Bread flour – 3 ¼ cups.
- Rosemary – ¼ cup., chopped
- Instant yeast – 1 ¼ tsp.

Directions:
1. Add all ingredients into the bread machine pan. Select sweet bread setting then select medium crust and start. Once loaf is done, remove the loaf pan from the machine. Allow it to cool for 10 minutes. Slice and serve.

89. Sauerkraut Rye Bread

Servings: 1 Loaf
Cooking Time: 10 Minutes
Ingredients:
- 12 slice bread (1½ pounds)
- 1 cup water, at 80°F to 90°F
- 1½ tablespoons melted butter, cooled
- ⅓ cup molasses
- ½ cup drained sauerkraut
- ⅓ teaspoon salt
- 1½ tablespoons unsweetened cocoa powder
- Pinch ground nutmeg
- ¾ cup rye flour
- 2 cups white bread flour
- 1⅔ teaspoons bread machine or instant yeast

Directions:
1. Preparing the Ingredients.
2. Choose the size of loaf of your preference and then measure the ingredients.
3. Add all of the ingredients mentioned previously in the list.
4. Close the lid after placing the pan in the bread machine.
5. Select the Bake cycle
6. Turn on the bread machine. Select the White/Basic setting, select the loaf size, and the crust color. Press start.
7. When the cycle is finished, carefully remove the pan from the bread maker and let it rest.
8. Remove the bread from the pan, put in a wire rack to Cool about 5 minutes. Slice

90. Honey Potato Flakes Bread

Servings: 1 Loaf
Ingredients:
- 16 slice bread (2 pounds)
- 1⅔ cups lukewarm milk
- 2⅔ tablespoons unsalted butter, melted
- 4 teaspoons honey
- 2 teaspoons table salt
- 4 cups white bread flour

- 1½ teaspoons dried thyme
- ⅔ cup instant potato flakes
- 2½ teaspoons bread machine yeast
- 12 slice bread (1½ pounds)
- 1¼ cups lukewarm milk
- 2 tablespoons unsalted butter, melted
- 1 tablespoon honey
- 1½ teaspoons table salt
- 3 cups white bread flour
- 1 teaspoon dried thyme
- ½ cup instant potato flakes
- 2 teaspoons bread machine yeast

Directions:
1. Choose the size of loaf you would like to make and measure your ingredients.
2. Add the ingredients to the bread pan in the order listed above.
3. Place the pan in the bread machine and close the lid.
4. Turn on the bread maker. Select the White/Basic setting, then the loaf size, and finally the crust color. Start the cycle.
5. When the cycle is finished and the bread is baked, carefully remove the pan from the machine. Use a potholder as the handle will be very hot. Let rest for a few minutes.
6. Remove the bread from the pan and allow to cool on a wire rack for at least 10 minutes before slicing.

Nutrition Info: (Per Serving):Calories 157, fat 3.1 g, carbs 27.8 g, sodium 294 mg, protein 4.8 g

91. Cinnamon Pull-apart Bread

Servings: 16
Cooking Time: 3 Hours
Ingredients:
- 1/3 cup whole milk
- 4 tablespoons unsalted butter
- 1/4 cup warm water
- 1 teaspoon pure vanilla extract
- 2 large eggs
- 3 cups all-purpose flour
- 1/4 cup sugar
- 1/2 teaspoon salt
- 2 1/4 teaspoons active dry yeast
- For the Filling:
- 4 tablespoons unsalted butter, melted until browned (will smell like warm caramel)
- 1 cup sugar
- 2 teaspoons ground cinnamon
- Pinch of ground nutmeg

Directions:
1. Add milk and butter to a saucepan and heat on medium-low until the butter melts; add liquid to the bread maker.
2. Add the rest of the ingredients (except yeast) in the order listed.
3. Make a well in the center of the dry ingredients and add the yeast.
4. Select Dough cycle and press Start.
5. When the dough is done, roll it out into a big sheet of dough, and brush the dough with the browned butter.
6. Combine sugar cinnamon and nutmeg in a mixing bowl and sprinkle over buttered dough.
7. Cut the dough into long thin strips and cut the strips into squares. Stack in threes, and place the dough squares next to one another in a greased bread pan.
8. Let rise in a warm place until doubled in size; cover with plastic wrap and refrigerate overnight to bake for breakfast.
9. Preheat an oven to 350°F.
10. Bake for 30 to 35 minutes, until the top is very golden brown.
11. When bread is done, transfer to a plate to cool and serve warm.

Nutrition Info: Calories: 210, Sodium: 126 mg, Dietary Fiber: 0.9 g, Fat: 6.8 g, Carbs: 34.3 g, Protein: 3.7 g.

92. Tomato Herb Bread

Servings: 1 Loaf
Cooking Time: 10 Minutes
Ingredients:
- 8 slice bread (1 pounds)
- ½ cup tomato sauce, at 80°F to 90°F
- ½ tablespoon olive oil
- ½ tablespoon sugar
- 1 tablespoon dried basil
- ½ tablespoon dried oregano
- ½ teaspoon salt
- 2 tablespoons grated Parmesan cheese
- 1½ cups white bread flour
- 1⅛ teaspoons bread machine or instant yeast

Directions:
1. Preparing the Ingredients.

2. Choose the size of loaf of your preference and then measure the ingredients.
3. Add all of the ingredients mentioned previously in the list.
4. Close the lid after placing the pan in the bread machine.
5. Select the Bake cycle
6. Turn on the bread machine. Select the White/Basic setting, select the loaf size, and the crust color. Press start.
7. When the cycle is finished, carefully remove the pan from the bread maker and let it rest.
8. Remove the bread from the pan, put in a wire rack to Cool about 5 minutes. Slice

93. Carrot Coriander Bread

Servings: 14 Slices
Cooking Time: 3 H.
Ingredients:
- 2-3 freshly grated carrots,
- 1⅛ cup lukewarm water
- 2 Tbsp sunflower oil
- 4 tsp freshly chopped coriander
- 2½ cups unbleached white bread flour
- 2 tsp ground coriander
- 1 tsp salt
- 5 tsp sugar
- 4 tsp easy blend dried yeast

Directions:
1. Add each ingredient to the bread machine in the order and at the temperature recommended by your bread machine manufacturer.
2. Close the lid, select the basic bread, medium crust setting on your bread machine, and press start.
3. When the bread machine has finished baking, remove the bread and put it on a cooling rack.

94. Potato Honey Bread

Servings: 1 Loaf
Cooking Time: 10 Minutes
Ingredients:
- 12 slice bread (1½ pounds)
- ¾ cup lukewarm water
- ½ cup finely mashed potatoes, at room temperature
- 1 egg, at room temperature
- ¼ cup unsalted butter, melted
- 2 tablespoons honey
- 1 teaspoon table salt
- 3 cups white bread flour
- 2 teaspoons bread machine yeast

Directions:
1. Preparing the Ingredients.
2. Choose the size of loaf of your preference and then measure the ingredients.
3. Add all of the ingredients mentioned previously in the list.
4. Close the lid after placing the pan in the bread machine.
5. Select the Bake cycle
6. Turn on the bread machine. Select the White/Basic setting, select the loaf size, and the crust color. Press start.
7. When the cycle is finished, carefully remove the pan from the bread maker and let it rest.
8. Remove the bread from the pan, put in a wire rack to Cool about 10 minutes.
9. Slice

95. Savory Sweet Potato Pan Bread

Servings: 1 Loaf
Cooking Time: 10 Minutes
Ingredients:
- 8 wedges
- 1½ cups uncooked shredded dark-orange sweet potato (about ½ potato) ½ cup sugar
- ¼ cup vegetable oil
- 2 eggs
- ¾ cup all-purpose flour
- ¾ cup whole wheat flour
- 2 teaspoons dried minced onion
- 1 teaspoon dried rosemary leaves, crumbled
- 1 teaspoon baking soda
- ½ teaspoon salt
- ¼ teaspoon baking powder
- 2 teaspoons sesame seed

Directions:
1. Preparing the Ingredients.
2. Choose the size of loaf of your preference and then measure the ingredients.
3. Add all of the ingredients mentioned previously in the list. Close the lid after placing the pan in the bread machine.
4. Select the Bake cycle
5. Turn on the bread machine. Select the White/Basic setting, select the loaf size, and the crust color. Press start.

6. When the cycle is finished, carefully remove the pan from the bread maker and let it rest.
7. Remove the bread from the pan, put in a wire rack to Cool about 10 minutes. Serve warm.

96. Pineapple Carrot Bread

Servings: 12 Slices
Cooking Time: 5 Minutes
Ingredients:
- 1 (8-ounce) can crushed pineapple, with juice
- 1/2 cup carrots, shredded
- 2 eggs
- 2 tablespoons butter
- 4 cups bread flour
- 3 tablespoons sugar
- 1 teaspoon salt
- 3/4 teaspoon ground ginger
- 1 1/4 teaspoons active dry yeast

Directions:
1. Preparing the Ingredients
2. Add all of the ingredients (except yeast) to the bread maker pan in the order listed above.
3. Make a well in the center of the dry ingredients and add the yeast.
4. Select the Bake cycle
5. Select the Basic bread cycle and press Start.
6. Transfer baked loaf to a cooling rack for 15 minutes before slicing to serve.

97. Blueberry Honey Bread

Servings: 1 Loaf
Cooking Time: 10 Minutes
Ingredients:
- 16 slice bread (2 pounds)
- 1 cup plain yogurt
- ⅔ cup lukewarm water
- ¼ cup honey
- 4 teaspoons unsalted butter, melted
- 2 teaspoons table salt
- 1½ teaspoons lime zest
- ⅔ teaspoon lemon extract
- 4 cups white bread flour
- 2¼ teaspoons bread machine yeast
- 1⅓ cups dried blueberries

Directions:
1. Preparing the Ingredients.
2. Choose the size of loaf of your preference and then measure the ingredients.
3. Add all of the ingredients mentioned previously in the list, except for the blueberries. Close the lid after placing the pan in the bread machine.
4. Select the Bake cycle
5. Turn on the bread machine. White/Basic or Fruit/Nut (if your machine has this setting) setting, select the loaf size, and the crust color. Press start.
6. When the machine signals to add ingredients, add the blueberries.
7. When the cycle is finished, carefully remove the pan from the bread maker and let it rest.
8. Remove the bread from the pan, put in a wire rack to cool for at least 10 minutes, and slice.

98. Cinnamon Raisin Breadsticks

Servings: 16
Cooking Time: 3 Hours
Ingredients:
- 1 cup milk
- 2 tablespoons water
- 1 tablespoon oil
- 3/4 teaspoon salt
- 2 tablespoons brown sugar
- 3 cups bread flour
- 1 teaspoon cinnamon
- 1 tablespoon active dry yeast
- 1/2 cup raisins
- Vanilla icing, for glaze

Directions:
1. Preheat oven to 475°F.
2. Mix the cinnamon into the bread flour.
3. Add milk, water, oil, salt and brown sugar to the bread maker pan, then add the flour/cinnamon mixture.
4. Make a well in the center of the dry ingredients and add the yeast.
5. Set on Dough cycle and press Start.
6. Take out the dough out and punch down; let rest for 10 minutes.
7. Roll dough into a 12-by-8-inch rectangle.
8. Sprinkle raisins on one half of the dough and gently press them into the dough.
9. Fold the dough in half and gently roll and stretch dough back out into a rectangle.
10. Cut into strips, then twist.
11. Line a baking sheet with parchment paper and bake for 4 minutes.
12. Place on 2 baking sheets that have been lined with parchment paper. Reduce oven temperature to 350°F.
13. Brush breadsticks lightly with water and return to oven and bake 20-25 minutes.

14. Cool on a wire rack.
15. Glaze with vanilla icing and serve.

Nutrition Info: Calories: 121, Sodium: 117 mg, Dietary Fiber: 1 g, Fat: 1.4 g, Carbs: 23.7 g, Protein: 3.4 g.

99. Zucchini Bread

Servings: 12 Slices
Cooking Time: 10 Minutes
Ingredients:
- 1/2 teaspoon salt
- 1 cup sugar
- 1 tablespoon pumpkin pie spice
- 1 tablespoon baking powder
- 1 teaspoon pure vanilla extract
- 1/3 cup milk
- 1/2 cup vegetable oil
- 2 eggs
- 2 cups bread flour
- 1 1/2 teaspoons active dry yeast or bread machine yeast
- 1 cup shredded zucchini, raw and unpeeled
- 1 cup of chopped walnuts (optional)

Directions:
1. Preparing the Ingredients
2. Add all of the ingredients for the zucchini bread into the bread maker pan in the order listed above, reserving yeast.
3. Make a well in the center of the dry ingredients and add the yeast.
4. Select the Bake cycle
5. Select Wheat bread cycle, medium crust color, and press Start.
6. Transfer to a cooling rack for 10 to 15 minutes before slicing to serve.

100. Australian Vegetable Bread

Servings: 8 Pcs
Cooking Time: 1 Hour And 50 Minutes
Ingredients:
- 4 cups (4 * 1 cup) all-purpose flour
- 4 tablespoons (4 * 1 tbsp) sugar
- 2 teaspoons (4 * ½ tsp) salt
- 2 tablespoons (4 * ½ tbsp) olive oil
- 1 teaspoon (4 * ¼ tsp) yeast
- liquid (3 parts juice + 1-part water)

Directions:
1. Knead in the bread maker four types of dough (3 species with different colors with juice and one kind with water). Take juices of mixed vegetables for colored liquid: for Bordeaux - juice of beet for red color - tomato juice for green color - juice or puree of spinach for white dough - water.
2. While the following kind of dough is kneaded, the previous lump stands warm to raise.
3. Use the Pasta Dough program on your bread maker.
4. The finished white dough was rolled into a large cake, the color dough of each kind was divided into four pieces each. In a white cake, lay the colored scones: roll them into small rolls and wrap them in 3 layers in a different order - you get four rolls. Then completely cover the colored cakes with white dough, create the desired form for the bucket, put it in the bread machine.
5. The program BAKING set the time to 60 minutes. The focus was that the loaf resembles plain white bread (as if bread with a surprise) However, the colored dough was foolish and sometimes decided to get out.

Nutrition Info: Calories 225;Total Fat 3.3g;Saturated Fat 0.5g;Cholesterol 0g;Sodium 466mg;Total Carbohydrate 43.1g;Dietary Fiber 1.4g

101. Light Corn Bread

Servings: 1 Loaf
Cooking Time: 10 Minutes
Ingredients:
- 12 slice bread (1½ pounds)
- ¾ cup milk, at 80°F to 90°F
- 1 egg, at room temperature
- 2¼ tablespoons butter, melted and cooled
- 2¼ tablespoons honey
- ¾ teaspoon salt
- ⅓ cup cornmeal
- 2⅔ cups white bread flour
- 1¾ teaspoons bread machine or instant yeast

Directions:
1. Preparing the Ingredients.
2. Choose the size of loaf of your preference and then measure the ingredients.
3. Add all of the ingredients mentioned previously in the list.
4. Close the lid after placing the pan in the bread machine.
5. Select the Bake cycle
6. Turn on the bread machine. Select the White/Basic setting, select the loaf size, and the crust color. Press start.
7. When the cycle is finished, carefully remove the pan from the bread maker and let it rest.

8. Remove the bread from the pan, put in a wire rack to Cool about 5 minutes. Slice

102. Cinnamon Apple Bread

Servings: 1 Loaf
Ingredients:
- 16 slice bread (2 pounds)
- 1⅓ cups lukewarm milk
- 3⅓ tablespoons butter, melted
- 2⅔ tablespoons sugar
- 2 teaspoons table salt
- 1⅓ teaspoons cinnamon, ground
- A pinch ground cloves
- 4 cups white bread flour
- 2¼ teaspoons bread machine yeast
- 1⅓ cups peeled apple, finely diced
- 12 slice bread (1½ pounds)
- 1 cup lukewarm milk
- 2½ tablespoons butter, melted
- 2 tablespoons sugar
- 1½ teaspoons table salt
- 1 teaspoon cinnamon, ground
- Pinch ground cloves
- 3 cups white bread flour
- 2¼ teaspoons bread machine yeast
- 1 cup peeled apple, finely diced

Directions:
1. Choose the size of loaf you would like to make and measure your ingredients.
2. Add all of the ingredients except for the apples to the bread pan in the order listed above.
3. Place the pan in the bread machine and close the lid.
4. Turn on the bread maker. Select the White/Basic or Fruit/Nut (if your machine has this setting) setting, then the loaf size, and finally the crust color. Start the cycle.
5. When the machine signals to add ingredients, add the apples. (Some machines have a fruit/nut hopper where you can add the apples when you start the machine. The machine will automatically add them to the dough during the baking process.)
6. When the cycle is finished and the bread is baked, carefully remove the pan from the machine. Use a potholder as the handle will be very hot. Let rest for a few minutes.
7. Remove the bread from the pan and allow to cool on a wire rack for at least 10 minutes before slicing.

Nutrition Info: (Per Serving):Calories 174, fat 2.3 g, carbs 26.4 g, sodium 286 mg, protein 4.6 g

103. Lemon-lime Blueberry Bread

Servings: 1 Loaf
Cooking Time: 10 Minutes
Ingredients:
- 12 slice bread (1½ pounds)
- ¾ cup plain yogurt, at room temperature
- ½ cup water, at 80°F to 90°F
- 3 tablespoons honey
- 1 tablespoon melted butter, cooled
- 1½ teaspoons salt
- ½ teaspoon lemon extract
- 1 teaspoon lime zest
- 1 cup dried blueberries
- 3 cups white bread flour
- 2¼ teaspoons bread machine or instant yeast

Directions:
1. Preparing the Ingredients.
2. Choose the size of loaf of your preference and then measure the ingredients.
3. Add all of the ingredients mentioned previously in the list. Close the lid after placing the pan in the bread machine
4. Select the Bake cycle
5. Turn on the bread machine. Select the White/Basic setting, select the loaf size, and the crust color. Press start.
6. When the cycle is finished, carefully remove the pan from the bread maker and let it rest.
7. Remove the bread from the pan, put in a wire rack to cool. Cool completely, about 10 minutes. Slice

CLASSIC DAILY BREAD

104. Whole Wheat Sunflower Bread

Servings: 1 Loaf
Ingredients:
- 16 slice bread (2 pounds)
- 1⅛ cups lukewarm water
- 2 tablespoons honey
- 2 tablespoons unsalted butter, melted
- 1 teaspoon table salt
- 3 cups whole-wheat flour
- 1 cup white bread flour
- 2 tablespoons sesame seeds
- ¼ cup raw sunflower seeds
- 2¼ teaspoons bread machine yeast
- 12 slice bread (1½ pounds)
- 1 cup lukewarm water
- 1½ tablespoons honey
- 1½ tablespoons unsalted butter, melted
- ¾ teaspoon table salt
- 2½ cups whole-wheat flour
- ¾ cup white bread flour
- 1 tablespoon sesame seeds
- 3 tablespoons raw sunflower seeds
- 1½ teaspoons bread machine yeast

Directions:
1. Choose the size of loaf you would like to make and measure your ingredients.
2. Add the ingredients to the bread pan in the order listed above.
3. Place the pan in the bread machine and close the lid.
4. Turn on the bread maker. Select the Whole Wheat/Wholegrain setting, then the loaf size, and finally the crust color. Start the cycle.
5. When the cycle is finished and the bread is baked, carefully remove the pan from the machine. Use a potholder as the handle will be very hot. Let rest for a few minutes.
6. Remove the bread from the pan and allow to cool on a wire rack for at least 10 minutes before slicing.

Nutrition Info: (Per Serving):Calories 253, fat 3.3 g, carbs 27.4 g, sodium 154 mg, protein 4.2 g

105. Garlic Pepperoni Bread

Servings: 14 Slices
Cooking Time: 3 H.
Ingredients:
- 1 cup water
- ¼ cup light olive oil
- 3 cups bread flour
- 1 Tbsp sugar
- 1 tsp salt
- ½-1 tsp garlic powder
- ½-1 Tbsp minced dried onions
- 1 tsp dried basil
- ¼ cup shredded mozzarella cheese
- ⅓ cup grated parmesan cheese
- ¼ cup pepperoni slice, chopped
- 2 tsp bread machine yeast

Directions:
1. Add each ingredient to the bread machine in the order and at the temperature recommended by your bread machine manufacturer.
2. Close the lid, select the basic bread, medium crust setting on your bread machine, and press start.
3. When the bread machine has finished baking, remove the bread and put it on a cooling rack.

106. Oat Molasses Bread

Servings: 1 Loaf
Ingredients:
- 16 slice bread (2 pounds)
- 1⅓ cups boiling water
- ¾ cup old-fashioned oats
- 3 tablespoons butter
- 1 large egg, lightly beaten
- 2 teaspoons table salt
- ¼ cup honey
- 1½ tablespoons dark molasses
- 4 cups white bread flour
- 2½ teaspoons bread machine yeast
- 12 slice bread (1½ pounds)
- 1 cup boiling water
- ½ cup old-fashioned oats
- 2 tablespoons butter
- 1 large egg, lightly beaten
- 1½ teaspoons table salt
- 3 tablespoons honey
- 1 tablespoon dark molasses
- 3 cups white bread flour
- 2 teaspoons bread machine yeast

Directions:
1. Add the boiling water and oats to a mixing bowl. Allow the oats to soak well and cool down completely. Do not drain the water.
2. Choose the size of loaf you would like to make and measure your ingredients.
3. Add the soaked oats, along with any remaining water, to the bread pan.
4. Add the remaining ingredients to the bread pan in the order listed above.
5. Place the pan in the bread machine and close the lid.
6. Turn on the bread maker. Select the White/Basic setting, then the loaf size, and finally the crust color. Start the cycle.
7. When the cycle is finished and the bread is baked, carefully remove the pan from the machine. Use a potholder as the handle will be very hot. Let rest for a few minutes.
8. Remove the bread from the pan and allow to cool on a wire rack for at least 10 minutes before slicing.

Nutrition Info: (Per Serving):Calories 160, fat 7.1 g, carbs 18 g, sodium 164 mg, protein 5.1 g

107. Banana Bread

Servings: 12
Cooking Time: 1 Hour And 20 Minutes
Ingredients:
- Eggs – 2
- Butter – 1/3 cup
- Milk – 1/8 cup
- Bananas – 2, mashed
- Bread flour – 1 1/3 cups
- Sugar – 2/3 cup
- Baking powder – 1 ¼ tsp.
- Baking soda – ½ tsp.
- Salt – ½ tsp.
- Chopped nuts – ½ cup, lightly toasted

Directions:
1. Add the butter, eggs, milk, and bananas to the bread pan and set aside.
2. Combine the remaining dry ingredients in a bowl and add the bread pan.
3. Use Quick Bread setting to bake the bread.
4. Remove the bread when done.
5. Slice and serve.

Nutrition Info: (Per Serving): Calories: 303; Total Fat: 17 g; Saturated Fat: 7 g; Carbohydrates: 33 g; Cholesterol: 14 mg; Fiber: 2 g; Calcium: 98 mg; Sodium: 523 mg; Protein: 7 g

108. Citrus And Walnut Bread

Servings: 14 Slices
Cooking Time: 3 H.
Ingredients:
- ¾ cup lemon yogurt
- ½ cup orange juice
- 5 tsp caster sugar
- 1 tsp salt
- 2.5 Tbsp butter
- 2 cups unbleached white bread flour
- 1½ tsp easy blend dried yeast
- ⅓ cup chopped walnuts
- 2 tsp grated lemon rind
- 2 tsp grated orange rind

Directions:
1. Add each ingredient except the walnuts and orange and lemon rind to the bread machine one by one, as per the manufacturer's instructions.
2. Close the lid, select the basic bread, medium crust setting on your bread machine, and press start.
3. Add the walnuts, and orange and lemon rind during the 2nd kneading cycle:
4. When the bread machine has finished baking, remove the bread and put it on a cooling rack.

109. Onion Bread

Servings: 12
Cooking Time: 3 Hours And 25 Minutes
Ingredients:
- Water – 1 ½ cup
- Butter – 2 tbsp. plus 2 tsp.
- Salt – 1 tsp.
- Sugar – 1 tbsp. plus 1 ½ tsp.
- Bread flour – 4 cups
- Nonfat dry milk – 2 tbsp. plus 2 tsp.
- Active dry yeast – 2 tsp.
- Dry onion soup mix – 4 tbsp.

Directions:
1. Place ingredients in the bread pan in the order listed, except the soup.
2. Select Basic cycle. Add the onion soup mix at the fruit and nut signal.
3. When done, remove and cool.
4. Slice and serve.

Nutrition Info: (Per Serving): Calories: 130; Total Fat: 3 g; Saturated Fat: 2 g; Carbohydrates: 16 g; Cholesterol: 8 mg; Fiber: 1 g; Calcium: 77 mg; Sodium: 843 mg; Protein: 8 g

110. Bread Machine Bread

Servings: 6
Cooking Time: 3 Hours And 25 Minutes
Ingredients:
- Flour – 2 cups, sifted
- Warm water – ¾ cup
- Sugar – 1 tsp.
- Active dry yeast – 1.25 tsp.
- Salt – 1 tsp.
- Oil – 1 tsp.

Directions:
1. Add ingredients according to bread machine recommendation.
2. Select the Basic setting and press Start.
3. Remove the loaf once it is baked.
4. Cool and slice.

Nutrition Info: (Per Serving): Calories: 163; Total Fat: 1 g; Saturated Fat: 0 g; Carbohydrates: 32 g; Cholesterol: 15 mg; Fiber: 1 g; Calcium: 18 mg; Sodium: 390 mg; Protein: 4 g

111. Flaxseed Milk Bread

Servings: 1 Loaf
Ingredients:
- 16 slice bread (2 pounds)
- 1½ cups lukewarm milk
- 2 tablespoons unsalted butter, melted
- 2 tablespoons honey
- 2 teaspoons table salt
- 4 cups white bread flour
- ½ cup flaxseed
- 1½ teaspoons bread machine yeast
- 12 slice bread (1½ pounds)
- 1⅛ cups lukewarm milk
- 1½ tablespoons unsalted butter, melted
- 1½ tablespoons honey
- 1 teaspoon table salt
- 3 cups white bread flour
- ¼ cup flaxseed
- 1¼ teaspoons bread machine yeast

Directions:
1. Choose the size of loaf you would like to make and measure your ingredients.
2. Add the ingredients to the bread pan in the order listed above.
3. Place the pan in the bread machine and close the lid.
4. Turn on the bread maker. Select the White/Basic setting, then the loaf size, and finally the crust color. Start the cycle.
5. When the cycle is finished and the bread is baked, carefully remove the pan from the machine. Use a potholder as the handle will be very hot. Let rest for a few minutes.
6. Remove the bread from the pan and allow to cool on a wire rack for at least 10 minutes before slicing.

Nutrition Info: (Per Serving):Calories 147, fat 3.2 g, carbs 27.4 g, sodium 216 mg, protein 5.8 g

112. Multigrain Honey Bread

Servings: 1 Loaf
Ingredients:
- 16 slice bread (2 pounds)
- 1½ cups lukewarm water
- 2 tablespoons unsalted butter, melted
- 1 tablespoon honey
- 1 teaspoon table salt
- 1½ cups multigrain flour
- 2¾ cups white bread flour
- 2 teaspoons bread machine yeast
- 12 slice bread (1½ pounds)
- 1⅛ cups lukewarm water
- 2 tablespoons unsalted butter, melted
- 1½ tablespoons honey
- 1½ teaspoons table salt
- 1⅛ cups multigrain flour
- 2 cups white bread flour
- 1½ teaspoons bread machine yeast

Directions:
1. Choose the size of loaf you would like to make and measure your ingredients.
2. Add the ingredients to the bread pan in the order listed above.
3. Place the pan in the bread machine and close the lid.
4. Turn on the bread maker. Select the White/Basic setting, then the loaf size, and finally the crust color. Start the cycle.
5. When the cycle is finished and the bread is baked, carefully remove the pan from the machine.

Use a potholder as the handle will be very hot. Let rest for a few minutes.

6. Remove the bread from the pan and allow to cool on a wire rack for at least 10 minutes before slicing.

Nutrition Info: (Per Serving):Calories 144, fat 2.2 g, carbs 26.3 g, sodium 287 mg, protein 4.1 g

113. Classic Corn Bread

Servings: 1 Loaf
Ingredients:
- 16 slice bread (2 pounds)
- 1⅓ cups lukewarm buttermilk
- ⅓ cup unsalted butter, melted
- 2 eggs, at room temperature
- ⅓ cup sugar
- 1½ teaspoons table salt
- 1⅔ cups all-purpose flour
- 1⅓ cups cornmeal
- 1⅓ tablespoon baking powder
- 12 slice bread (1½ pounds)
- 1 cup lukewarm buttermilk
- ¼ cup unsalted butter, melted
- 2 eggs, at room temperature
- ¼ cup sugar
- 1 teaspoon table salt
- 1⅓ cups all-purpose flour
- 1 cup cornmeal
- 1 tablespoon baking powder

Directions:
1. Choose the size of loaf you would like to make and measure your ingredients.
2. Add the ingredients to the bread pan in the order listed above.
3. Place the pan in the bread machine and close the lid.
4. Turn on the bread maker. Select the Quick/Rapid setting, then the loaf size, and finally the crust color. Start the cycle.
5. When the cycle is finished and the bread is baked, carefully remove the pan from the machine. Use a potholder as the handle will be very hot. Let rest for a few minutes.
6. Remove the bread from the pan and allow to cool on a wire rack for at least 10 minutes before slicing.

Nutrition Info: (Per Serving):Calories 157, fat 5.2 g, carbs 23.8 g, sodium 257 mg, protein 4.1 g

114. 10 Minute Rosemary Bread

Servings: 12
Cooking Time: 2 Hours
Ingredients:
- 1 cup warm water, about 105°F
- 2 tablespoons butter, softened
- 1 egg
- 3 cups all-purpose flour
- ¼ cup whole wheat flour
- ⅓ cup sugar
- 1 teaspoon salt
- 3 teaspoons bread maker yeast
- 2 tablespoons rosemary, freshly chopped
- For the topping:
- 1 egg, room temperature
- 1 teaspoon milk, room temperature
- Garlic powder
- Sea salt

Directions:
1. Place all of the ingredients in the bread maker pan in the order listed above.
2. Select Dough cycle.
3. When dough is kneaded, place on parchment paper on a flat surface and roll into two loaves; set aside and allow to rise for 30 minutes.
4. Preheat a pizza stone in an oven on 375°F for 30 minutes.
5. For the topping, add the egg and milk to a small mixing bowl and whisk to create an egg wash. Baste the formed loaves and sprinkle evenly with garlic powder and sea salt.
6. Allow to rise for 40 minutes, lightly covered, in a warm area.
7. Bake for 15 to 18 minutes or until golden brown. Serve warm.

Nutrition Info: Calories: 176, Sodium: 220 mg, Dietary Fiber: 1.5 g, Fat: 3.1 g, Carbs: 32 g, Protein: 5 g.

115. Cranberry Walnut Bread

Servings: 14 Slices
Cooking Time: 3 H.
Ingredients:
- ¼ cup water
- 1 egg
- 3 Tbsp honey
- 1½ tsp butter, softened
- 3¼ cups bread flour

- 1 cup milk
- 1 tsp salt
- ¼ tsp baking soda
- 1 tsp ground cinnamon
- 2½ tsp active dry yeast
- ¾ cup dried cranberries
- ½ cup chopped walnuts
- 1 Tbsp white vinegar
- ½ tsp sugar

Directions:
1. Add each ingredient except the berries and nuts to the bread machine in the order and at the temperature recommended by your bread machine manufacturer.
2. Close the lid, select the basic bread, medium crust setting on your bread machine, and press start.
3. Add the cranberries and walnuts around 5 minutes before the kneading cycle has finished
4. When the bread machine has finished baking, remove the bread and put it on a cooling rack.

116. Classic White Bread Ii

Servings: 1 Loaf
Ingredients:
- 16 slice bread (2 pounds)
- 1 1/2 cups water, lukewarm between 80 and 90°F
- 3 tablespoons unsalted butter, melted
- 1 tablespoon sugar
- 3 tablespoons dry milk powder
- 1 1/4 teaspoons table salt
- 4 cup white bread flour
- 1 1/2 teaspoons bread machine yeast
- 12 slice bread (1 ½ pounds)
- 1 1/4 cups water, lukewarm between 80 and 90°F
- 2 tablespoons unsalted butter, melted
- 2 teaspoons sugar
- 2 tablespoons dry milk powder
- 1 teaspoons table salt
- 3 1/4 cup white bread flour
- 1 1/4 teaspoons bread machine yeast

Directions:
1. Choose the size of loaf you would like to make and measure your ingredients.
2. Add the ingredients to the bread pan in the order listed above.
3. Place the pan in the bread machine and close the lid.
4. Turn on the bread maker. Select the White/Basic setting, then the loaf size, and finally the crust color. Start the cycle.
5. When the cycle is finished and the bread is baked, carefully remove the pan from the machine. Use a potholder as the handle will be very hot. Let rest for a few minutes.
6. Remove the bread from the pan and allow to cool on a wire rack for at least 10 minutes before slicing.

Nutrition Info: (Per Serving):Calories 148, fat 3.6 g, carbs 23.4 g, sodium 197 mg, protein 3.4 g

117. French Crusty Loaf Bread

Servings: 1 Loaf
Ingredients:
- 16 slice bread (2 pounds)
- 2 cups + 2 tablespoons water, lukewarm between 80 and 90°F
- 4 teaspoons sugar
- 2 teaspoons table salt
- 6 1/2 cups white bread flour
- 2 teaspoons bread machine yeast
- 12 slice bread (1 ½ pounds)
- 1 1/2 cups + 1 tablespoon water, lukewarm between 80 and 90°F
- 3 teaspoons sugar
- 1 1/2 teaspoons table salt
- 4 3/4 cups white bread flour
- 1 1/2 teaspoons bread machine yeast

Directions:
1. Choose the size of loaf you would like to make and measure your ingredients.
2. Add the ingredients to the bread pan in the order listed above.
3. Place the pan in the bread machine and close the lid.
4. Turn on the bread maker. Select the French setting, then the loaf size, and finally the crust color. Start the cycle.
5. When the cycle is finished and the bread is baked, carefully remove the pan from the machine. Use a potholder as the handle will be very hot. Let rest for a few minutes.
6. Remove the bread from the pan and allow to cool on a wire rack for at least 10 minutes before slicing.

Nutrition Info: (Per Serving):Calories 186, fat 1.2 g, carbs 31.4 g, sodium 126 mg, protein 5.7 g

118. Julekake

Servings: 14 Slices
Cooking Time: 3 H.
Ingredients:
- ⅓ cup evaporated milk
- ⅔ cup water
- 1 egg, room temperature
- 3⅓ cups bread flour
- ¼ cup sugar
- ½ tsp salt
- ½ tsp cardamom
- ½ cup softened butter, cut up
- 2¼ tsp dry active yeast
- ½ cup golden raisins
- ⅔ cup candied fruit

Directions:
1. Add each ingredient except the raisins to the bread machine in the order and at the temperature recommended by your bread machine manufacturer.
2. Close the lid, select the basic bread, low crust setting on your bread machine, and press start.
3. Add the raisins and fruit about 5 minutes before the kneading cycle has finished.
4. When the bread machine has finished baking, remove the bread and put it on a cooling rack.

119. Cinnamon Rolls

Servings: 12 Rolls
Cooking Time: 2 H.
Ingredients:
- For the cinnamon roll dough:
- 1 cup milk
- 1 large egg
- 4 Tbsp butter
- 3⅓ cups bread flour
- 3 Tbsp sugar
- ½ tsp salt
- 2 tsp active dry yeast
- For the filling:
- ¼ cup butter, melted
- ¼ cup sugar
- 2 tsp cinnamon
- ½ tsp nutmeg
- ⅓ cup nuts, chopped and toasted
- For the icing:
- 1 cup powdered sugar
- 1 - 2 Tbsp milk
- ½ tsp vanilla

Directions:
1. Add each ingredient to the bread machine in the order and at the temperature recommended by your bread machine manufacturer.
2. Select the dough cycle and press start.
3. When it's done, transfer the dough onto a floured surface.
4. Knead it for 1 minute, then let it rest for the next 15 minutes.
5. Roll out a rectangle. Spread ¼ cup of melted butter over the dough.
6. Sprinkle the dough with cinnamon, ¼ cup sugar, nutmeg, and nuts.
7. Roll the dough, beginning from a long side. Seal the edges and form an evenly shaped roll. Cut it into 1-inch pieces.
8. Put them on a greased baking pan.
9. Cover with towel and leave for 45 minutes to rise.
10. Bake at 375°F in a preheated oven for 20-25 minutes.
11. Remove from the oven. Cool for 10 minutes.
12. Mix the icing ingredients in a bowl. Adjust with sugar or milk to desired thickness.
13. Cover the rolls with icing and serve.

120. Pumpernickel Bread

Servings: 1 Loaf
Ingredients:
- 16 slice bread (2 pounds)
- 1 1/3 cups water, lukewarm between 80 and 90°F
- 2 large eggs, room temperature and not cold
- ¼ cup oil
- ¼ cup honey
- 3 tablespoons dry milk powder
- ¼ cup cocoa powder
- 3 tablespoons caraway seeds
- 1 tablespoon instant coffee granules
- 2 teaspoons table salt
- 1 cup rye flour
- 1 cup whole wheat bread flour
- 2 cups white bread flour
- 2 ¼ teaspoons bread machine yeast
- 12 slice bread (1 ½ pounds)

- 3/4 cups water, lukewarm between 80 and 90°F
- 2 large eggs, room temperature and not cold
- 2 tablespoons oil
- 2 tablespoons honey
- 3 tablespoons dry milk powder
- 3 tablespoons cocoa powder
- 2 tablespoons caraway seeds
- 2 teaspoon instant coffee granules
- 1 1/2 teaspoons table salt
- 3/4 cup rye flour
- 3/4 cup whole wheat bread flour
- 1 1/2 cups white bread flour
- 1 3/4 teaspoons bread machine yeast

Directions:
1. Choose the size of loaf you would like to make and measure your ingredients. If you want to make a 1-pound or 2 ½-pound loaf, please adjust your ingredient quantities accordingly. You can look at the conversion table at the end of the book for easy adjustments or click here.
2. Take the bread pan; add the ingredients in order listed above.
3. Secure the pan into the bread machine and close the lid.
4. Power the bread maker and select the option of the bread – White/Basic – then the size of the loaf you are making, and finally the crust color you desire. Start the machine.
5. After the bread cycle is done and the bread is cooked, carefully remove the pan from the machine. Use a potholder as the handle will be very hot. Let rest for a few minutes.
6. Remove the bread from the pan and allow to cool down on a wired rack for at least 10 minutes or more before slicing.

Nutrition Info: (Per Serving):Calories 134, fat 3.1 g, carbs 19 g, sodium 143 mg, protein 4.2 g

121. Buttermilk Bread

Servings: 1 Loaf
Ingredients:
- 16 slice bread (2 pounds)
- 1¼ cups lukewarm buttermilk
- 2 tablespoons unsalted butter, melted
- 2 tablespoons sugar
- 1½ teaspoons table salt
- ½ teaspoon baking powder
- 3½ cups white bread flour
- 2¼ teaspoons bread machine yeast
- 12 slice bread (1½ pounds)
- 1¼ cups lukewarm buttermilk
- 1½ tablespoons unsalted butter, melted
- 1½ tablespoons sugar
- 1⅛ teaspoons table salt
- ⅓ teaspoon baking powder
- 2⅔ cups white bread flour
- 1⅔ teaspoons bread machine yeast

Directions:
1. Choose the size of loaf you would like to make and measure your ingredients.
2. Add the ingredients to the bread pan in the order listed above.
3. Place the pan in the bread machine and close the lid.
4. Turn on the bread maker. Select the White/Basic setting, then the loaf size, and finally the crust color. Start the cycle.
5. When the cycle is finished and the bread is baked, carefully remove the pan from the machine. Use a potholder as the handle will be very hot. Let rest for a few minutes.
6. Remove the bread from the pan and allow to cool on a wire rack for at least 10 minutes before slicing.

Nutrition Info: (Per Serving):Calories 132, fat 2.2 g, carbs 23.4 g, sodium 234 mg, protein 4.3 g

122. Classic Dark Bread

Servings: 1 Loaf
Ingredients:
- 16 slice bread (2 pounds)
- 1¼ cups lukewarm water
- 2 tablespoons unsalted butter, melted
- ½ cup molasses
- ½ teaspoon table salt
- 1 cup rye flour
- 2½ cups white bread flour
- 2 tablespoons unsweetened cocoa powder
- Pinch ground nutmeg
- 2¼ teaspoons bread machine yeast
- 12 slice bread (1½ pounds)
- 1 cup lukewarm water
- 1½ tablespoons unsalted butter, melted
- ⅓ cup molasses
- ⅓ teaspoon table salt
- ¾ cup rye flour

- 2 cups white bread flour
- 1½ tablespoons unsweetened cocoa powder
- Pinch ground nutmeg
- 1⅔ teaspoons bread machine yeast

Directions:
1. Choose the size of loaf you would like to make and measure your ingredients.
2. Add the ingredients to the bread pan in the order listed above.
3. Place the pan in the bread machine and close the lid.
4. Turn on the bread maker. Select the White/Basic setting, then the loaf size, and finally the crust color. Start the cycle.
5. When the cycle is finished and the bread is baked, carefully remove the pan from the machine. Use a potholder as the handle will be very hot. Let rest for a few minutes.
6. Remove the bread from the pan and allow to cool on a wire rack for at least 10 minutes before slicing.

Nutrition Info: (Per Serving):Calories 143, fat 2.3 g, carbs 28.6 g, sodium 237 mg, protein 3.8 g

123. Pizza Rolls

Servings: 15
Cooking Time: 3 Hours
Ingredients:
- 1 cup warm water
- 3 tablespoons olive oil
- 3 cups bread flour
- 3 tablespoons sugar
- 1 1/2 teaspoons salt
- 2 1/4 teaspoons instant yeast
- For the Filling:
- 1 package pepperoni, sliced
- 1 bag mozzarella cheese, shredded
- 1 cup pizza sauce
- 1 jar of mild banana pepper rings

Directions:
1. Add the liquid ingredients to your bread maker first, then add flour and salt.
2. Create a small hole in the flour and add the sugar and yeast.
3. Select the Dough cycle and press Start.
4. Once your dough has fully risen, lay it out on a lightly floured surface, and punch it back down.
5. Knead by hand for about 30 seconds; be sure not to overwork the dough.
6. Pinch off a small amount of dough and flatten out into the shape of a circle and baste with one teaspoon of sauce. Layer with three slices of pepperoni, a good pinch of cheese, and a few banana pepper rings.
7. Fold one side over to the other and pinch the seams together, creating a seal. Fold corners over and do the same; repeat until all dough is used.
8. Place rolls on a large 9-by-13-inch baking sheet and bake at 350°F for about 25 mins or until slightly golden brown.
9. Remove rolls and allow to cool on a cooling rack for 10 to 15 minutes before eating; serve warm.

Nutrition Info: Calories: 142, Sodium: 329 mg, Dietary Fiber: 1.1 g, Fat: 3.7 g, Carbs: 23.7 g, Protein: 3.7 g.

124. Garlic Cheese Pull-apart Rolls

Servings: 12 - 24
Cooking Time: 3 Hours
Ingredients:
- 1 cup water
- 3 cups bread flour
- 1 1/2 teaspoons salt
- 1-1/2 tablespoons butter
- 3 tablespoons sugar
- 2 tablespoons nonfat dry milk powder
- 2 teaspoons yeast
- For the topping:
- 1/4 cup butter, melted
- 1 garlic clove, crushed
- 2 tablespoons parmesan cheese, plus more if needed
- Flour, for surface

Directions:
1. Place first 6 ingredients in bread maker pan in order listed.
2. Make a well in the flour; pour the yeast into the hole.
3. Select Dough cycle, press Start.
4. Turn finished dough onto a floured countertop.
5. Gently roll and stretch dough into a 24-inch rope.
6. Grease a 13-by-9-inch baking sheet.
7. Divide dough into 24 pieces with a sharp knife and shape into balls; place on prepared pan. Combine butter and garlic in a small mixing bowl and pour over rolls.
8. Sprinkle rolls evenly with parmesan cheese.

9. Cover and let rise for 30-45 minutes until doubled.
10. Bake at 375°F for 10 to 15 minutes or until golden brown.
11. Remove from oven, pull apart, and serve warm.
Nutrition Info: Calories: 109, Sodium: 210 mg, Dietary Fiber: 0.6 g, Fat: 3.5 g, Carbs: 16.7 g, Protein: 2.6 g.

125. Rosemary Focaccia Bread

Servings: 4 - 6
Cooking Time: 3 Hours
Ingredients:
- 1 cup, plus 3 tablespoons water
- 1 tablespoon extra-virgin olive oil
- 1 teaspoon salt
- 2 teaspoons fresh rosemary, chopped
- 3 cups bread flour
- 1 1/2 teaspoons instant yeast
- For the topping:
- 3 tablespoons olive oil
- Coarse salt
- Red pepper flakes

Directions:
1. Add water, oil, salt, rosemary, and flour to the bread maker pan.
2. Make a well in the center of the dry ingredients and add the yeast.
3. Select Dough cycle and press Start.
4. Transfer finished dough to a floured surface.
5. Cover and let rest for 5 minutes.
6. Form dough into a smooth ball and roll into a 12-inch round.
7. Place on a 12-inch pizza pan that has been lightly greased with olive oil. Poke dough randomly with fingertips to form dimples. Brush top with olive oil and sprinkle with salt and red pepper flakes to taste.
8. Let rise uncovered in warm, draft-free space for about 30 minutes.
9. Bake at 425°F for 18 to 22 minutes or until done.
10. Serve warm.
Nutrition Info: Calories: 312, Sodium: 390 mg, Dietary Fiber: 2.1 g, Fat: 10.1 g, Carbs: 48.3 g, Protein: 6.9 g.

126. Lemon Cake

Servings: 12
Cooking Time: 2 Hours 50 Minutes
Ingredients:
- 3 large eggs, beaten
- 1/3 cup 2% milk
- 1/2 cup butter, melted
- 2 cups all-purpose flour
- 3 teaspoons baking powder
- 1 1/3 cup sugar
- 1 teaspoon vanilla extract
- 2 lemons, zested
- For the glaze:
- 1 cup powdered sugar
- 2 tablespoons lemon juice, freshly squeezed

Directions:
1. Prepare the glaze by whisking the powdered sugar and lemon juice together in a small mixing bowl and set aside.
2. Add all of the remaining ingredients to the baking pan in the order listed.
3. Select the Sweet bread, medium color crust, and press Start.
4. When baked, transfer the baking pan to a cooling rack.
5. When the cake has cooled completely, gently shake the cake out onto a serving plate. Glaze the cool cake and serve.
Nutrition Info: Calories: 290, Sodium: 77 mg, Dietary Fiber: 0.6 g, Fat: 9.3 g, Carbs: 42.9 g, Protein: 4 g.

127. Fat-free Whole Wheat Bread

Servings: 12
Cooking Time: 1 Hour And 20 Minutes
Ingredients:
- Water – 1 7/8 cup
- White whole wheat flour – 4 2/3 cups
- Vital wheat gluten – 4 tbsp.
- Sugar – 2 tbsp.
- Salt – 1 ½ tsp.
- Rapid rise yeast – 2 ½ tsp.

Directions:
1. Add the water in the bread machine pan.
2. Add the remaining ingredients according to bread machine recommendation.
3. Choose Quick-Bake Whole Wheat cycle and press Start.
4. Remove the bread when complete.
5. Cool, slice, and serve.

Nutrition Info: (Per Serving): Calories: 134; Total Fat: 0.6 g; Saturated Fat: 0 g; Carbohydrates: 27.6 g; Cholesterol: 11 mg; Fiber: 6.5 g; Calcium: 18 mg; Sodium: 221.5 mg; Protein: 6.5 g

128. Basic Seed Bread

Servings: 1 Loaf
Ingredients:
- 16 slice bread (2 pounds)
- 1½ cups lukewarm water
- 2 tablespoons unsalted butter, melted
- 2 tablespoons sugar
- 1½ teaspoons table salt
- 3¼ cups white bread flour
- ¾ cup ground chia seeds
- 2 tablespoons sesame seeds
- 2 teaspoons bread machine yeast
- 12 slice bread (1½ pounds)
- 1⅛ cups lukewarm water
- 1½ tablespoons unsalted butter, melted
- 1½ tablespoons sugar
- 1⅛ teaspoons table salt
- 2½ cups white bread flour
- ½ cup ground chia seeds
- 1½ tablespoons sesame seeds
- 1½ teaspoons bread machine yeast

Directions:
1. Choose the size of loaf you would like to make and measure your ingredients.
2. Add the ingredients to the bread pan in the order listed above.
3. Place the pan in the bread machine and close the lid.
4. Turn on the bread maker. Select the White/Basic setting, then the loaf size, and finally the crust color. Start the cycle.
5. When the cycle is finished and the bread is baked, carefully remove the pan from the machine. Use a potholder as the handle will be very hot. Let rest for a few minutes.
6. Remove the bread from the pan and allow to cool on a wire rack for at least 10 minutes before slicing.

Nutrition Info: (Per Serving):Calories 153, fat 2.3 g, carbs 24.8 g, sodium 208 mg, protein 5.3 g

129. Pumpkin Spice Cake

Servings: 12
Cooking Time: 2 Hours 50 Minutes
Ingredients:
- 1 cup sugar
- 1 cup canned pumpkin
- 1/3 cup vegetable oil
- 1 teaspoon vanilla extract
- 2 eggs
- 1 1/2 cups all-purpose flour
- 2 teaspoons baking powder
- 1/4 teaspoon salt
- 1 teaspoon ground cinnamon
- 1/4 teaspoon ground nutmeg
- 1/8 teaspoon ground cloves
- Shortening, for greasing pan

Directions:
1. Grease bread maker pan and kneading blade generously with shortening.
2. Add all ingredients to the bread maker pan in the order listed above.
3. Select Rapid cycle and press Start.
4. Open the lid three minutes into the cycle and carefully scrape down sides of pan with a rubber spatula; close lid to continue cycle.
5. Cool baked cake for 10 minutes on a wire rack before slicing.

Nutrition Info: Calories: 195, Sodium: 64 mg, Dietary Fiber: 1.3 g, Fat: 7.1 g, Carbs: 31.2 g, Protein: 2.8 g.

130. Cinnamon Pecan Coffee Cake

Servings: 10 - 12
Cooking Time: 2 Hours
Ingredients:
- 1 cup butter, unsalted
- 1 cup sugar
- 2 eggs
- 1 cup sour cream
- 1 teaspoon vanilla extract
- 2 cups all-purpose flour
- 1 teaspoon baking powder
- 1 teaspoon baking soda
- 1/2 teaspoon salt
- For the topping:
- 1/2 cup brown sugar
- 1/4 cup sugar
- 1/2 teaspoon cinnamon
- 1/2 cup pecans, chopped

Directions:

1. Add butter, sugar, eggs, sour cream and vanilla to the bread maker baking pan, followed by the dry ingredients.
2. Select Cake cycle and press Start.
3. Prepare topping and set aside.
4. When kneading cycle is done, after about 20 minutes, sprinkle 1/2 cup of topping on top of dough and continue baking.
5. During the last hour of baking time, sprinkle the remaining 1/2 cup of topping on the cake. Bake until complete. Cool on a wire rack for 10 minutes and serve warm.

Nutrition Info: Calories: 488, Sodium: 333 mg, Dietary Fiber: 2.5 g, Fat: 32.8 g, Carbs: 46.4 g, Protein: 5.7 g.

131. Honey Pound Cake

Servings: 12 - 16
Cooking Time: 2 Hours 50 Minutes
Ingredients:
- 1 cup butter, unsalted
- 1/4 cup honey
- 2 tablespoons whole milk
- 4 eggs, beaten
- 1 cup sugar
- 2 cups flour

Directions:
1. Bring the butter to room temperature and cut into 1/2-inch cubes.
2. Add the ingredients to the bread machine in the order listed (butter, honey, milk, eggs, sugar, flour).
3. Press Sweet bread setting, light crust color, and press Start.
4. Take the cake out of the bread pan using a rubber spatula, as soon as it's finished. Cool on a rack and serve with your favorite fruit.

Nutrition Info: Calories: 117, Sodium: 183 mg, Dietary Fiber: 0.3 g, Fat: 6.9 g, Carbs: 12.3 g, Protein: 1.9 g.

132. Oat Bran Molasses Bread

Servings: 8
Cooking Time: 3 Hours And 48 Minutes
Ingredients:
- Water - 1/2 cup
- Melted butter - 1½ tbsp., cooled
- Blackstrap molasses - 2 tbsp.
- Salt - 1/4 tsp.
- Ground nutmeg - 1/8 tsp.
- Oat bran - 1/2 cup
- Whole-wheat bread flour - 1½ cups
- Bread machine or instant yeast - 1⅛ tsp.

Directions:
1. Place the ingredients in the bread machine according to instructions.
2. Choose Whole-Wheat/Whole-Grain bread, and Light or Medium crust. Press Start.
3. Remove when done and cool. Slice and serve.

Nutrition Info: (Per Serving): Calories: 137; Total Fat: 3 g; Saturated Fat: 2 g; Carbohydrates: 25 g; Cholesterol: 15 mg; Fiber: 1 g; Calcium: 20 mg; Sodium: 112 mg; Protein: 3 g

133. Pepperoni Bread

Servings: 10
Cooking Time: 3 Hours 10 Minutes
Ingredients:
- 1 cup plus 2 tablespoons warm water
- 1/3 cup mozzarella cheese, shredded
- 2 tablespoons sugar
- 1 1/2 teaspoons garlic salt
- 1 1/2 teaspoons dried oregano
- 3 1/4 cups bread flour
- 1 1/2 teaspoons active dry yeast
- 2/3 cup sliced pepperoni

Directions:
1. Add the first six ingredients in order listed above, reserving the yeast.
2. Make a well in the flour; pour the yeast into the hole.
3. Select Basic bread setting, medium crust color, and press Start.
4. Check dough after 5 minutes of mixing and add 1 to 2 tablespoons of water or flour if needed. Just before the final kneading, add the pepperoni.
5. Remove loaf when finished and allow to cool for 10 to 15 minutes on a cooling rack before serving.

Nutrition Info: Calories: 165, Sodium: 13 mg, Dietary Fiber: 1.4 g, Fat: 0.8 g, Carbs: 34.1 g, Protein: 4.9 g.

134. Honey Nut Bread

Servings: 8
Cooking Time: 3 Hours And 25 Minutes
Ingredients:
- Eggs – 2

- Cottage cheese – 2/3 cup
- Milk – ½ cup
- Butter – ¼ cup
- Honey – 2 tbsp.
- All-purpose flour – 4 cups
- Instant yeast – 1 tbsp.
- Salt – 1 tsp.
- Candied nuts – ¾ cups, chopped

Directions:
1. Add everything, except nuts to your bread machine according to manufacturer recommendation.
2. Select Basic and choose Light crust type. Press Start.
3. Add the nuts when the machine beeps.
4. Remove the bread when ready.
5. Cool, slice, and serve.

Nutrition Info: (Per Serving): Calories: 422; Total Fat: 13.9 g; Saturated Fat: 5.2 g; Carbohydrates: 59.8 g; Cholesterol: 59 mg; Fiber: 2.8 g; Calcium: 62 mg; Sodium: 450 mg; Protein: 13.7 g

135. Blue Cheese Bread

Servings: 10 - 12
Cooking Time: 3 Hours

Ingredients:
- 3/4 cup warm water
- 1 large egg
- 1 teaspoon salt
- 3 cups bread flour
- 1 cup blue cheese, crumbled
- 2 tablespoons nonfat dry milk
- 2 tablespoons sugar
- 1 teaspoon bread machine yeast

Directions:
1. Add the ingredients to bread machine pan in the order listed above, (except yeast) ; be sure to add the cheese with the flour.
2. Make a well in the flour; pour the yeast into the hole.
3. Select Basic bread cycle, medium crust color, and press Start.
4. When finished, transfer to a cooling rack for 10 minutes and serve warm.

Nutrition Info: Calories: 171, Sodium: 266 mg, Dietary Fiber: 0.9 g, Fat: 3.9 g, Carbs: 26.8 g, Protein: 6.7 g.

136. Oat Quinoa Bread

Servings: 1 Loaf

Ingredients:
- 16 slice bread (2 pounds)
- 1⅓ cups lukewarm milk
- ¾ cup cooked quinoa, cooled
- 5 tablespoons unsalted butter, melted
- 4 teaspoons sugar
- 1⅓ teaspoons table salt
- 2 cups white bread flour
- 5 tablespoons quick oats
- 1 cup whole-wheat flour
- 2 teaspoons bread machine yeast
- 12 slice bread (1½ pounds)
- 1 cup lukewarm milk
- ⅔ cup cooked quinoa, cooled
- ¼ cup unsalted butter, melted
- 1 tablespoon sugar
- 1 teaspoon table salt
- 1½ cups white bread flour
- ¼ cup quick oats
- ¾ cup whole-wheat flour
- 1½ teaspoons bread machine yeast

Directions:
1. Choose the size of loaf you would like to make and measure your ingredients.
2. Add the ingredients to the bread pan in the order listed above.
3. Place the pan in the bread machine and close the lid.
4. Turn on the bread maker. Select the White/Basic setting, then the loaf size, and finally the crust color. Start the cycle.
5. When the cycle is finished and the bread is baked, carefully remove the pan from the machine. Use a potholder as the handle will be very hot. Let rest for a few minutes.
6. Remove the bread from the pan and allow to cool on a wire rack for at least 10 minutes before slicing.

Nutrition Info: (Per Serving):Calories 153, fat 5.3 g, carbs 22.3 g, sodium 238 mg, protein 3.8 g

137. Rye Bread

Servings: 1 Loaf

Ingredients:
- 16 slice bread (2 pounds)
- 1⅔ cups lukewarm water

- ¼ cup + 4 teaspoons Dijon mustard
- 2 tablespoons unsalted butter, melted
- 4 teaspoons sugar
- 1 teaspoon table salt
- 2 cups rye flour
- 2⅔ cups white bread flour
- 1½ teaspoons bread machine yeast
- 12 slice bread (1½ pounds)
- 1¼ cups lukewarm water
- ¼ cup Dijon mustard
- 1½ tablespoons unsalted butter, melted
- 1 tablespoon sugar
- ¾ teaspoon table salt
- 1½ cups rye flour
- 2 cups white bread flour
- 1 teaspoon bread machine yeast

Directions:
1. Choose the size of loaf you would like to make and measure your ingredients.
2. Add the ingredients to the bread pan in the order listed above.
3. Place the pan in the bread machine and close the lid.
4. Turn on the bread maker. Select the White/Basic setting, then the loaf size, and finally the crust color. Start the cycle.
5. When the cycle is finished and the bread is baked, carefully remove the pan from the machine. Use a potholder as the handle will be very hot. Let rest for a few minutes.
6. Remove the bread from the pan and allow to cool on a wire rack for at least 10 minutes before slicing.

Nutrition Info: (Per Serving):Calories 153, fat 2.1 g, carbs 24.8 g, sodium 256 mg, protein 5.2 g

138. Savory Bread Maker Rolls

Servings: 24
Cooking Time: 2 Hours 10 Mins
Ingredients:
- 1 cup warm milk, 70° to 80°F
- 1/2 cup butter, softened
- 1/4 cup sugar
- 2 eggs
- 1 1/2 teaspoons salt
- 4 cups bread flour
- 2 tablespoons herbes de Provence
- 2 1/4 teaspoons active dry yeast
- Flour, for surface

Directions:
1. Add all ingredients in the order listed above to the bread maker pan, reserving yeast.
2. Make a well in the flour; add yeast to the hole.
3. Select Dough setting; when Dough cycle is completed, turn dough out onto a lightly floured surface.
4. Divide dough into 24 portions and shape into balls.
5. Place rolls in a greased 13-by-9-inch baking pan.
6. Cover and let rise in a warm place for 30-45 minutes; preheat an oven to 350°F.
7. Bake for 13-16 minutes or until golden brown and serve warm.

Nutrition Info: Calories: 129, Sodium: 185 mg, Dietary Fiber: 0.6 g, Fat: 4.6 g, Carbs: 18.7 g, Protein: 3.1 g.

139. Italian Easter Cake

Servings: 4 Slices
Cooking Time: 3 H.
Ingredients:
- 1¾ cups wheat flour
- 2½ Tbsp quick-acting dry yeast
- 8 Tbsp sugar
- ½ tsp salt
- 3 chicken eggs
- ¾ cup milk
- 3 Tbsp butter
- 1 cup raisins

Directions:
1. Add each ingredient except the raisins to the bread machine in the order and at the temperature recommended by your bread machine manufacturer.
2. Close the lid, select the sweet loaf, low crust setting on your bread machine, and press start.
3. When the dough is kneading, add the raisins.
4. When the bread machine has finished baking, remove the bread and put it on a cooling rack.

140. Honey Sunflower Bread

Servings: 1 Loaf
Ingredients:
- 16 slice bread (2 pounds)
- 1⅓ cups lukewarm water
- 2 eggs, at room temperature

- ¼ cup unsalted butter, melted
- ¼ cup skim milk powder
- 2 tablespoons honey
- 2 teaspoons table salt
- 4 cups white bread flour
- 1 cup raw sunflower seeds
- 1¾ teaspoons bread machine yeast
- 12 slice bread (1½ pounds)
- 1 cup lukewarm water
- 1 egg, at room temperature
- 3 tablespoons unsalted butter, melted
- 3 tablespoons skim milk powder
- 1½ tablespoons honey
- 1½ teaspoons table salt
- 3 cups white bread flour
- ¾ cup raw sunflower seeds
- 1 teaspoon bread machine yeast

Directions:
1. Choose the size of loaf you would like to make and measure your ingredients.
2. Add the ingredients to the bread pan in the order listed above.
3. Place the pan in the bread machine and close the lid.
4. Turn on the bread maker. Select the White/Basic setting, then the loaf size, and finally the crust color. Start the cycle.
5. When the cycle is finished and the bread is baked, carefully remove the pan from the machine. Use a potholder as the handle will be very hot. Let rest for a few minutes.
6. Remove the bread from the pan and allow to cool on a wire rack for at least 10 minutes before slicing.

Nutrition Info: (Per Serving):Calories 172, fat 4.7 g, carbs 27.8 g, sodium 324 mg, protein 4.9 g

141. Whole Wheat Corn Bread

Servings: 1 Loaf
Ingredients:
- 16 slice bread (2 pounds)
- 1⅓ cups lukewarm water
- 2 tablespoons light brown sugar
- 1 large egg, beaten
- 2 tablespoons unsalted butter, melted
- 1½ teaspoons table salt
- ¾ cup whole wheat flour
- ¾ cup cornmeal
- 2¾ cups white bread flour
- 2½ teaspoons bread machine yeast
- 12 slice bread (1½ pounds)
- 1 cup lukewarm water
- 1½ tablespoons light brown sugar
- 1 medium egg, beaten
- 1½ tablespoons unsalted butter, melted
- 1½ teaspoons table salt
- ½ cup whole wheat flour
- ½ cup cornmeal
- 2 cups white bread flour
- 1½ teaspoons bread machine yeast

Directions:
1. Choose the size of loaf you would like to make and measure your ingredients.
2. Add the ingredients to the bread pan in the order listed above.
3. Place the pan in the bread machine and close the lid.
4. Turn on the bread maker. Select the White/Basic setting, then the loaf size, and finally the crust color. Start the cycle.
5. When the cycle is finished and the bread is baked, carefully remove the pan from the machine. Use a potholder as the handle will be very hot. Let rest for a few minutes.
6. Remove the bread from the pan and allow to cool on a wire rack for at least 10 minutes before slicing.

Nutrition Info: (Per Serving):Calories 146, fat 5.7 g, carbs 19.3 g, sodium 124 mg, protein 4.8 g

142. Rainbow Swirl Cake

Servings: 15
Cooking Time: 3 Hours
Ingredients:
- 1 cup milk plus 1 egg yolk
- 3 cups unbleached all-purpose flour
- 2 1/2 tablespoons sugar
- 2 1/4 teaspoons active dry yeast
- 1 1/2 tablespoons unsalted butter, softened
- 2 teaspoons salt
- Red, yellow, green and blue food coloring
- Flour, for surface

Directions:
1. Whisk milk and egg yolk together in a microwave safe bowl and microwave 30 seconds; add to bread maker pan.

2. Whisk together flour, sugar and yeast in a large mixing bowl and add to bread maker pan.
3. Add milk mixture, butter, salt, and stir to combine; add to bread maker pan.
4. Select Dough cycle and press Start.
5. When kneading is finished, divide dough into 5 equal dough balls and place each one in a small bowl and cover with a tea towel.
6. Remove one piece from a bowl and place it on a plastic cutting board. Add several drops of food coloring and knead the food coloring into the dough with gloved hands, adding more food coloring until it is fully incorporated.
7. Shape dough into a ball and return to its bowl. Repeat with remaining pieces of dough, dying each a different color; be sure to wash your hands and your work surface between each color.
8. Cover each bowl with plastic wrap and let rise until doubled; about 2 hours.
9. Punch down each dough ball when risen.
10. Roll the red dough ball out on a lightly floured surface into an 8-by-4-inch rectangle. Roll out yellow piece of dough into an 8-by-4-inch rectangle and place directly on top of the red dough. Repeat with green, blue, and purple dough balls until you have a stack of 8-by-4-inch rectangles.
11. Roll up dough tightly from the short end into a loaf.
12. Place loaf in a lightly greased 9-by-5-inch loaf pan. Cover with a tea towel or plastic wrap and let rise until doubled, about 1 hour.
13. Preheat oven to 375°F and bake until browned on top and a thermometer inserted in the bottom center reads 190°F, about 30 minutes.
14. Remove loaf from pan and cool completely on a wirerack before slicing.

Nutrition Info: Calories: 122, Sodium: 327 mg, Dietary Fiber: 0.8 g, Fat: 2.1 g, Carbs: 22.2 g, Protein: 3.5 g.

143. Christmas Bread

Servings: 8 Slices
Cooking Time: 3 H.
Ingredients:
- 1¼ cups warm whole milk (70°F to 80°F)
- ½ tsp lemon juice
- 2 Tbsp butter, softened
- 2 Tbsp sugar
- 1½ tsp salt
- 3 cups bread flour
- 2 tsp active dry yeast
- ¾ cup golden raisins
- ¾ cup raisins
- ½ cup dried currants
- 1½ tsp grated lemon zest
- Glaze:
- ½ cup powdered sugar
- 1½ tsp 2% milk
- 1 tsp melted butter
- ¼ tsp vanilla extract

Directions:
1. Add each ingredient except the raisins, currants, and lemon zest to the bread machine in the order and at the temperature recommended by your bread machine manufacturer.
2. Close the lid, select the sweet loaf, low crust setting on your bread machine, and press start.
3. Just before the final kneading, add the raisins, currants and lemon zest.
4. When the bread machine has finished baking, remove the bread and put it on a cooling rack.
5. Combine the glaze ingredients in a bowl.
6. Drizzle over the cooled bread.

144. Apple Pecan Cinnamon Rolls

Servings: 12 Rolls
Cooking Time: 3 H.
Ingredients:
- 1 cup warm milk (70°F to 80°F)
- 2 large eggs
- ⅓ cup butter, melted
- ½ cup sugar
- 1 tsp salt
- 4½ cups bread flour
- 2½ tsp bread machine yeast
- For the filling:
- 3 Tbsp butter, melted
- 1 cup finely chopped peeled apples
- ¾ cup packed brown sugar
- ⅓ cup chopped pecans
- 2½ tsp ground cinnamon
- For the icing:
- 1½ cup confectioners sugar
- ⅜ cup cream cheese, softened
- ¼ cup butter, softened
- ½ tsp vanilla extract
- ⅛ tsp salt drained

Directions:

1. Add each ingredient for the dough to the bread machine in order stipulated by the manufacturer.
2. Set to dough cycle and press start.
3. When cycle has completed, place the dough onto a well-floured surface. Roll it into a rectangle. Brush it with butter.
4. Mix the brown sugar, apples, pecans, and cinnamon in a bowl. Spread over the dough evenly.
5. Beginning from the long side, roll the dough. Cut it into 1¾-inch slices.
6. Transfer them onto a greased baking dish. Cover and let rise for 30 minutes.
7. Bake at 325°F in a preheated oven for 25-30 minutes.
8. Meanwhile, mix all the icing ingredients in a bowl.
9. Take out the rolls and let them cool
10. Cover warm rolls with the glaze and serve.

145. Coffee Rye Bread

Servings: 6
Cooking Time: 3 Hours And 25 Minutes
Ingredients:
- Lukewarm water – ½ cup
- Brewed coffee – ¼ cup, 80°F
- Dark molasses – 2 tbsp.
- Brown sugar – 5 tsp.
- Unsalted butter – 4 tsp., softened
- Powdered skim milk – 1 tbsp.
- Kosher salt – 1 tsp.
- Unsweetened cocoa powder – 4 tsp.
- Dark rye flour – 2/3 cup
- Whole-wheat bread machine flour – ½ cup
- Caraway seeds – 1 tsp.
- White bread machine flour – 1 cup
- Bread machine yeast – 1 ½ tsp

Directions:
1. Place everything in the bread machine pan according to the bread machine recommendation.
2. Select Basic and Light crust. Press Start.
3. Remove the bread.
4. Cool, slice, and serve.

Nutrition Info: (Per Serving): Calories: 222; Total Fat: 3.2 g; Saturated Fat: 1.8 g; Carbohydrates: 42.9 g; Cholesterol: 8 mg; Fiber: 4.7 g; Calcium: 40 mg; Sodium: 415 mg; Protein: 6.3 g

146. Classic White Sandwich Bread

Servings: 1 Loaf
Ingredients:
- 16 slice bread (2 pounds)
- 1 cup water, lukewarm between 80 and 90°F
- 2 tablespoons unsalted butter, melted
- 1 teaspoon table salt
- 1/4 cup sugar
- 2 egg whites or 1 egg, beaten
- 3 cups white bread flour
- 1 1/2 teaspoons bread machine yeast
- 12 slice bread (1 ½ pounds)
- 3/4 cup water, lukewarm between 80 and 90°F
- 1 1/2 tablespoons unsalted butter, melted
- 3/4 teaspoon table salt
- 1 ½ ounces sugar
- 2 egg whites or 1 egg, beaten
- 2 1/4 cups white bread flour
- 1 1/8 teaspoons bread machine yeast

Directions:
1. Choose the size of loaf you would like to make and measure your ingredients.
2. Add the ingredients to the bread pan in the order listed above.
3. Place the pan in the bread machine and close the lid.
4. Turn on the bread maker. Select the White/Basic setting, then the loaf size, and finally the crust color. Start the cycle.
5. When the cycle is finished and the bread is baked, carefully remove the pan from the machine. Use a potholder as the handle will be very hot. Let rest for a few minutes.
6. Remove the bread from the pan and allow to cool on a wire rack for at least 10 minutes before slicing.

Nutrition Info: (Per Serving):Calories 126, fat 2.3 g, carbs 23 g, sodium 137 mg, protein 4 g

147. Baguette Style French Bread

Servings: 2 Loaves
Ingredients:
- 2 baguettes of 1-pound each
- 1 ⅔ cups water, lukewarm between 80 and 90°F
- 1 teaspoon table salt
- 4 ⅔ cups white bread flour

- 2 ⅔ teaspoons bread machine yeast or rapid rise yeast
- 2 baguettes of ¾-pound each
- 1 ¼ cups water, lukewarm between 80 and 90°F
- ¾ teaspoon table salt
- 3 ½ cups white bread flour
- 2 teaspoons bread machine yeast or rapid rise yeast
- Other Ingredients:
- Cornmeal
- Olive oil
- 1 egg white
- 1 tablespoon water

Directions:
1. Choose the size of crusty bread you would like to make and measure your ingredients.
2. Add the ingredients for the bread machine to the bread pan in the order listed above.
3. Place the pan in the bread machine and close the lid. Turn on the bread maker. Select the dough/manual setting.
4. When the dough cycle is completed, remove the pan and lay the dough on a floured working surface.
5. Knead the dough a few times and add flour if needed so the dough is not too sticky to handle. Cut the dough in half and form a ball with each half.
6. Grease a baking sheet with olive oil. Dust lightly with cornmeal.
7. Preheat the oven to 375° and place the oven rack in the middle position.
8. With a rolling pin dusted with flour, roll one of the dough balls into a 12-inch by 9 -inch rectangle for the 2 pounds bread size or a 10-inch by 8-inch rectangle for the 1 ½ pound bread size. Starting on the longer side, roll the dough tightly. Pinch the ends and the seam with your fingers to seal. Roll the dough in a back in forth movement to make it into a nice French baguette shape.
9. Repeat the process with the second dough ball.
10. Place loaves of bread onto the baking sheet with the seams down and brush with some olive oil with enough space in between them to rise. Dust top of both loaves with a little bit of cornmeal. Cover with a clean kitchen towel and place in a warm area with any air draught. Let rise for 10 to 15 minutes, or until loaves doubled in size.
11. Mix the egg white and 1 tablespoon of water and lightly brush over both loaves of bread.
12. Place in the oven and bake for 20 minutes. Remove from oven and brush with remaining egg wash on top of both loaves of bread. Place back into the oven taking care of turning around the baking sheet. Bake for another 5 to 10 minutes or until the baguettes are golden brown. Let rest on a wired rack for 5-10 minutes before serving.

Nutrition Info: (Per Serving):Calories 87, fat 0.8 g, carbs 16.5 g, sodium 192 mg, protein 3.4 g

148. Panettone

Servings: 14 Slices
Cooking Time: 3 H. 10 Min.
Ingredients:
- ¾ cup warm water
- 6 Tbsp vegetable oil
- 1½ tsp salt
- 4 Tbsp sugar
- 2 eggs
- 3 cups bread flour
- 1 (¼ ounce) package Fleishman's yeast
- ½ cup candied fruit
- ⅓ cup chopped almonds
- ½ tsp almond extract

Directions:
1. Add each ingredient to the bread machine in the order and at the temperature recommended by your bread machine manufacturer.
2. Close the lid, select the sweet loaf, low crust setting on your bread machine, and press start.
3. When the bread machine has finished baking, remove the bread and put it on a cooling rack.

149. German Butter Cake

Servings: 12 - 16
Cooking Time: 2 Hour 25 Minutes
Ingredients:
- 2 teaspoons active dry yeast
- 1/4 cup sugar
- 2 1/4 cups all-purpose flour
- 1 teaspoon salt
- 7/8 cup whole milk, lukewarm
- 1 egg yolk
- 1 tablespoon butter, softened
- For the topping:
- 3 tablespoons butter, cold
- 1/2 cup almonds, sliced

- 1/3 cup sugar

Directions:
1. Add all of the dough ingredients to the bread maker pan.
2. Press Dough cycle and Start.
3. Grease a 10-inch springform pan; when the dough cycle is finished, pat the dough into the pan.
4. Prepare the topping by cutting the butter into -inch squares and place them sporadically over the surface of the dough, slightly pushing each into the dough.
5. Sprinkle with almond slices, then sprinkle evenly with sugar.
6. Cover with a towel and let stand in a warm place for 30 minutes.
7. Preheat an oven to 375 F.
8. Bake for 20 to 25 minutes or until golden brown.
9. Let cool 10 minutes in pan on cooling rack and serve warm!

Nutrition Info: Calories: 226, Sodium: 228 mg, Dietary Fiber: 1 g, Fat: 9.1 g, Carbs: 29.8 g, Protein: 7.1 g.

150. Donuts

Servings: 24
Cooking Time: 55 Minutes
Ingredients:
- 1 1/4 cups whole milk
- 1 beaten egg
- 1/4 cup shortening
- 1/4 cup sugar
- 1 teaspoon salt
- 3 1/2 cups all-purpose flour
- 1 1/2 teaspoons dry yeast

Directions:
1. Measure ingredients into the bread maker, first adding wet then dry ingredients as listed above, reserving yeast.
2. Make a well in the flour; pour the yeast into the hole.
3. Select Dough cycle and press Start.
4. Roll kneaded dough out to a 1/2-inch thick rectangle and cut with a 2 1/2 inch donut cutter.
5. Let rise, covered, for 30 minutes or until doubled in size.
6. Preheat a deep fryer to 375°F.
7. Drop donuts into fryer and turn donuts as they rise to the surface. Fry until golden brown.
8. Drain on paper towels to cool. Glaze or dust with your favorite donut topping while warm and serve.

Nutrition Info: Calories: 104, Sodium: 105 mg, Dietary Fiber: 0.5 g, Fat: 3 g, Carbs: 16.7 g, Protein: 2.7 g.

151. Chocolate Chip Bread

Servings: 14 Slices
Cooking Time: 3 H.
Ingredients:
- ¼ cup water
- 1 cup milk
- 1 egg
- 3 cups bread flour
- 3 Tbsp brown sugar
- 2 Tbsp white sugar
- 1 tsp salt
- 1 tsp ground cinnamon
- 1½ tsp active dry yeast
- 2 Tbsp margarine, softened
- ¾ cup semisweet chocolate chips

Directions:
1. Add each ingredient except the chocolate chips to the bread machine in the order and at the temperature recommended by your bread machine manufacturer.
2. Close the lid, select the sweet loaf, low crust setting on your bread machine, and press start.
3. Add the chocolate chips about 5 minutes before the kneading cycle has finished.
4. When the bread machine has finished baking, remove the bread and put it on a cooling rack.

152. Lemon Blueberry Quick Bread

Servings: 10 - 12
Cooking Time: 2 Hours
Ingredients:
- 2 cups all-purpose flour
- 1 1/2 teaspoons baking powder
- 1/2 teaspoon salt
- 1 tablespoon lemon zest
- 1 cup sugar
- 1/2 cup unsalted butter, softened
- 2 large eggs
- 2 teaspoons pure vanilla extract
- 1/2 cup whole milk
- 1 1/2 cups blueberries
- For the crumb topping:

- 1/3 cup sugar
- 3 tablespoons all-purpose flour
- 2 tablespoons butter, melted
- Non-stick cooking spray

Directions:
1. Spray bread maker pan with non-stick cooking spray and lightly flour.
2. Combine crumb topping ingredients and set aside.
3. In a small bowl, whisk together flour, baking powder and salt and set aside.
4. In a large mixing bowl, combine sugar and lemon zest. Add butter and beat until light and fluffy. Add eggs, vanilla and milk.
5. Add flour mixture and mix just until combine. Stir in blueberries and spread batter evenly into bread maker pan.
6. Top with crumb topping; select Sweet bread, light color crust, and press Start.
7. When done cool on a wire rack for 15 minutes and serve warm.

Nutrition Info: Calories: 462, Sodium: 332 mg, Dietary Fiber: 1 g, Fat: 32.1 g, Carbs: 41.8 g, Protein: 4 g.

153. Parsley And Chive Pull-apart Rolls

Servings: 16
Cooking Time: 3 Hours
Ingredients:
- 1 cup buttermilk
- 6 tablespoons unsalted butter, cut into 6 pieces
- 3 2/3 cups all-purpose flour
- 2 1/4 teaspoons instant yeast
- 1/3 cup granulated sugar
- 1 teaspoon salt
- 3 large egg yolks
- 1/4 cup chives, chopped
- 1/4 cup parsley, chopped
- For the topping:
- 1/4 cup butter, melted

Directions:
1. Combine the buttermilk and the 6 tablespoons butter in a small saucepan and warm until the butter melts, stirring continuously. Add the packet of instant yeast and allow to stand for five minutes.
2. Mix the egg yolks with a fork and add to the above mixture and blend.
3. Combine the flour, sugar, salt and herbs.
4. Add first the wet then the dry ingredients to your bread machine.
5. Set on Dough cycle and press Start.
6. Lightly grease a 9-by-13-inch glass baking dish.
7. Turn the dough out onto a clean work surface and press down gently. If the dough is too sticky add a little flour to the work surface. Using a bench scraper or a chef's knife, divide the dough into 16 equal pieces
8. Work one piece of dough at a time into a ball; keep the others covered with plastic wrap until ready to bake.
9. Cover the entire baking dish with plastic wrap and let the balls rise in a warm space, about 40 to 60 minutes.
10. Preheat an oven to 375°F and bake 20 to 25 minutes, or until lightly golden brown.
11. Remove from the oven and brush the tops with melted butter, serve warm.

Nutrition Info: Calories: 196, Sodium: 201 mg, Dietary Fiber: 0.9 g, Fat: 8.4 g, Carbs: 26.5 g, Protein: 3.8 g.

154. Oat Bran Nutmeg Bread

Servings: 1 Loaf
Ingredients:
- 16 slice bread (2 pounds)
- 1 cup lukewarm water
- 3 tablespoons unsalted butter, melted
- ¼ cup blackstrap molasses
- ½ teaspoon table salt
- 3 cups whole-wheat bread flour
- ¼ teaspoon ground nutmeg
- 1 cup oat bran
- 2¼ teaspoons bread machine yeast
- 12 slice bread (1½ pounds)
- ¾ cup lukewarm water
- 2¼ tablespoons unsalted butter, melted
- 3 tablespoons blackstrap molasses
- ⅓ teaspoon table salt
- 2¼ cups whole-wheat bread flour
- ¼ teaspoon ground nutmeg
- ¾ cup oat bran
- 1⅔ teaspoons bread machine yeast

Directions:
1. Choose the size of loaf you would like to make and measure your ingredients.
2. Add the ingredients to the bread pan in the order listed above.

3. Place the pan in the bread machine and close the lid.
4. Turn on the bread maker. Select the Whole Wheat/Wholegrain setting, then the loaf size, and finally the crust color. Start the cycle.
5. When the cycle is finished and the bread is baked, carefully remove the pan from the machine. Use a potholder as the handle will be very hot. Let rest for a few minutes.
6. Remove the bread from the pan and allow to cool on a wire rack for at least 10 minutes before slicing.

Nutrition Info: (Per Serving):Calories 141, fat 2.8 g, carbs 23.6 g, sodium 124 mg, protein 3.4 g

155. Chocolate Coffee Bread

Servings: 14 Slices
Cooking Time: 3 H.

Ingredients:
- 1⅓ cups water
- ⅓ cup cocoa powder
- 1⅓ cups bread flour
- 1⅓ cups whole wheat flour
- 3 Tbsp powdered milk
- ½ tsp salt
- 1½ Tbsp honey
- 2 envelopes instant mocha cappuccino mix
- 2¼ tsp active dry yeast
- ½ cup semi-sweet chocolate chips

Directions:
1. Add each ingredient except chips and mocha mix to the bread machine in the order and at the temperature recommended by your bread machine manufacturer.
2. Close the lid, select the sweet loaf, low crust setting on your bread machine, and press start.
3. Add the chocolate chips and mocha mix about 5 minutes before the kneading cycle has finished.
4. When the bread machine has finished baking, remove the bread and put it on a cooling rack.

BASIC BREAD

156. Hawaiian Sandwich Bread

Servings: 14 Slices
Cooking Time: 3 H.
Ingredients:
- ¾ cup pineapple juice
- 1 egg
- 2½ Tbsp olive oil
- 4 level Tbsp sugar
- 1 tsp kosher salt
- 3 level cups bread flour
- ½ cup milk
- 2 level tsp quick rise yeast

Directions:
1. Add each ingredient to the bread machine in the order and at the temperature recommended by your bread machine manufacturer.
2. Close the lid, select the basic bread, low crust setting on your bread machine and press start.
3. When the bread machine has finished baking, remove the bread and put it on a cooling rack.

157. Coconut Flour Bread

Servings: 12 Pcs
Cooking Time: 15 Minutes
Ingredients:
- 6 eggs
- 1/2 cup coconut flour
- 2 tbsp psyllium husk
- 1/4 cup olive oil
- 1 1/2 tsp salt
- 1 tbsp xanthan gum
- 1 tbsp baking powder
- 2 1/4 tsp yeast

Directions:
1. Use a small bowl to combine all of the dry ingredients except for the yeast.
2. In the bread machine pan, add all the wet ingredients.
3. Add all of your dry ingredients from the small mixing bowl to the bread machine pan. Top with the yeast.
4. Set the machine to the basic setting.
5. When the bread is finished, remove the bread machine pan from the bread machine.
6. Let cool slightly before transferring to a cooling rack.
7. It can be stored for four days on the counter and up to 3 months in the freezer.

Nutrition Info: Calories: 174 ;Carbohydrates: 4g ;Protein: 7g ;Fat: 15g

158. Perfect Sandwich Bread

Servings: 10
Cooking Time: 2 Hours
Ingredients:
- All-purpose flour – 4 cups
- Olive oil – 2 tbsps.
- Yeast – 2 tsps.
- Honey – 1 ½ tsp.
- Warm water – 1 ¾ cups
- Salt – 1 tsp

Directions:
1. Add water, honey, salt, olive oil, flour, and yeast into the bread machine pan. Select basic/white bread setting then select light/medium crust and start. Once loaf is done, remove the loaf pan from the machine. Allow it to cool for 5 minutes. Slice and serve.

159. Vegan White Bread

Servings: 14 Slices
Cooking Time: 3 H.
Ingredients:
- 1⅓ cups water
- ⅓ cup plant milk (I use silk soy original)
- 1½ tsp salt
- 2 Tbsp granulated sugar
- 2 Tbsp vegetable oil
- 3½ cups all-purpose flour
- 1¾ tsp bread machine yeast

Directions:
1. Add each ingredient to the bread machine in the order and at the temperature recommended by your bread machine manufacturer.
2. Close the lid, select the basic or white bread, medium crust setting on your bread machine, and press start.
3. When the bread machine has finished baking, remove the bread and put it on a cooling rack.

160. Warm Spiced Pumpkin Bread

Servings: One Loaf (12 Slices)
Cooking Time: 60 To 75 Minutes
Ingredients:

- 1½ cups pumpkin purée
- Three eggs, at room temperature
- 1/3 cup melted butter cooled
- 1 cup of sugar
- 3 cups all-purpose flour
- 1½ teaspoons baking powder
- ¾ teaspoon ground cinnamon
- ½ teaspoon baking soda
- ¼ teaspoon ground nutmeg
- ¼ teaspoon ground ginger
- ¼ teaspoon salt
- Pinch ground cloves

Directions:
1. Lightly grease the bread bucket with butter.
2. Add the pumpkin, eggs, butter, and sugar.
3. Program the machine for Quick/Rapid setting and press Start.
4. Let the wet ingredients be mixed by the paddles until the first fast mixing cycle is finished, about 10 minutes into the process.
5. While the wet ingredients are mixing
6. stir together the flour, baking powder, cinnamon, baking soda, nutmeg
7. ginger, salt, and cloves until well blended.
8. Add the dry ingredients to the bucket when the second fast mixing cycle starts.
9. Scrape down the sides of the bucket once after the dry ingredients are mixed into the wet.
10. When the loaf is finished, remove the bucket from the machine.
11. Let it cool for five minutes.
12. Gently shake the bucket to remove the bread and turn it out onto a rack to cool.

Nutrition Info: Calories: 251;Fat: 7g ;Carbohydrates: 43g;Fibre: 2g;Sodium: 159mg;Protein: 5g

161. Extra Buttery White Bread

Servings: 16 Slices
Cooking Time: 3 H. 10 Min.
Ingredients:
- 1⅛ cups milk
- 4 Tbsp unsalted butter
- 3 cups bread flour
- 1½ Tbsp white granulated sugar
- 1½ tsp salt
- 1½ tsp bread machine yeast

Directions:
1. Soften the butter in your microwave.
2. Add each ingredient to the bread machine in the order and at the temperature recommended by your bread machine manufacturer.
3. Close the lid, select the basic or white bread, medium crust setting on your bread machine, and press start.
4. When the bread machine has finished baking, remove the bread and put it on a cooling rack.

162. Oatmeal Walnut Bread

Servings: 1 Loaf
Cooking Time: 1 Hour And 30 Minutes
Ingredients:
- ¾ cup whole-wheat flour
- ¼ cup all-purpose flour
- ½ cup brown sugar
- 1/3 cup walnuts, chopped
- ¼ cup oatmeal
- ¼ teaspoon of baking soda
- Two tablespoons baking powder
- One teaspoon salt
- 1 cup Vegan buttermilk
- ¼ cup of vegetable oil
- Three tablespoons aquafaba

Directions:
1. Add into the bread pan the wet ingredients then followed by the dry ingredients.
2. Use the "Quick" or "Cake" setting of your bread machine.
3. Allow the cycles to be completed.
4. Take out the pan from the machine.
5. Wait for 10 minutes, then remove the bread from the pan.
6. Once the bread has cooled down, slice it and serve.

Nutrition Info: Calories: 80;Carbohydrates: 11g;Fat: 3g;Protein: 2g

163. Luscious White Bread

Servings: 10
Cooking Time: 2 Hours
Ingredients:
- Warm milk – 1 cup.
- Eggs – 2
- Butter – 2 ½ tbsps.
- Sugar – ¼ cup.
- Salt – ¾ tsp.
- Bread flour – 3 cups.
- Yeast – 2 ½ tsps.

Directions:
1. Add all ingredients to the bread machine pan according to the bread machine manufacturer instructions. Select basic bread setting then select light crust and start. Once loaf is done, remove the loaf pan from the machine. Allow it to cool for 10 minutes. Slice and serve.

164. Homemade Hot Dog And Hamburger Buns

Servings: 8 - 10
Cooking Time: 1 Hour 35 Minutes
Ingredients:
- 1 1/4 cups milk, slightly warmed
- 1 egg, beaten
- 2 tablespoons butter, unsalted
- 1/4 cup white sugar
- 3/4 teaspoon salt
- 3 3/4 cups bread flour
- 1 1/4 teaspoons active dry yeast
- Flour, for surface

Directions:
1. Place all ingredients into the pan of the bread maker in the following order, reserving yeast: milk, egg, butter, sugar, salt, flour.
2. Make a well in the center of the dry ingredients and add the yeast.
3. Select Dough cycle. When cycle is complete, turn out onto floured surface.
4. Cut dough in half and roll each half out to a 1" thick circle.
5. Cut each half into 6 (3 1/2") rounds with inverted glass as a cutter. (For hot dog buns, cut lengthwise into 1-inch-thick rolls, and cut a slit along the length of the bun for easier separation later.)
6. Place on a greased baking sheet far apart and brush with melted butter.
7. Cover and let rise until doubled, about one hour; preheat an oven to 350°F.
8. Bake for 9 minutes.
9. Let cool and serve with your favorite meats and toppings!

Nutrition Info: Calories: 233, Sodium: 212 mg, Dietary Fiber: 1.4 g, Fat: 3.8 g, Carbs: 42.5 g, Protein: 6.6 g.

165. Autumn Treasures Loaf

Servings: 1 Loaf
Cooking Time: 1 Hour And 30 Minutes
Ingredients:
- 1 cup all-purpose flour
- ½ cup dried fruit, chopped
- ¼ cup pecans, chopped
- ¼ cup of sugar
- Two tablespoons baking powder
- One teaspoon salt
- ¼ teaspoon of baking soda
- ½ teaspoon ground nutmeg
- 1 cup apple juice
- ¼ cup of vegetable oil
- Three tablespoons aquafaba
- One teaspoon of vanilla extract

Directions:
1. Add all wet ingredients first to the bread pan before the dry ingredients.
2. Turn on the bread machine with the "Quick" or "Cake" setting.
3. Wait for all cycles to be finished.
4. Remove the bread pan from the machine.
5. After 10 minutes, transfer the bread from the pan into a wire rack.
6. Slice the bread only when it has completely cooled down.

Nutrition Info: Calories: 80;Carbohydrates: 12g;Fat: 3g;Protein: 1g

166. Vegan Cinnamon Raisin Bread

Servings: 1 Loaf
Cooking Time: 3 Hours
Ingredients:
- Two ¼ cups oat flour
- ¾ cup raisins
- ½ cup almond flour
- ¼ cup of coconut sugar
- 2 ½ teaspoons cinnamon
- One teaspoon baking powder
- ½ teaspoon baking soda
- ¼ teaspoon salt
- ¾ cup of water
- ½ cup of soy milk
- ¼ cup maple syrup
- Three tablespoons coconut oil
- One teaspoon vanilla extract

Directions:
1. Put all wet ingredients first into the bread pan, followed by the dry ingredients.

2. Set the bread machine to "Quick" or "Cake" mode.
3. Wait until the mixing and baking cycles are done.
4. Remove the pan from the machine.
5. Wait for another 10 minutes before transferring the bread to a wire rack.
6. After the bread has completely cooled down, slice it and serve.
Nutrition Info: Calories: 130;Carbohydrates: 26g;Fat: 2g;Protein: 3g

167. Traditional Italian Bread

Servings: 1 Loaf
Cooking Time: 10 Minutes
Ingredients:
- 12 slice bread (1½ pounds)
- 1 cup water, at 80°F to 90°F
- 1½ tablespoons olive oil
- 1½ tablespoons sugar
- 1⅛ teaspoons salt
- 3 cups white bread flour
- 2⅔ cups white bread flour
- 1½ teaspoons bread machine or instant yeast

Directions:
1. Preparing the Ingredients.
2. Place the ingredients in your bread machine as recommended by the manufacturer
3. Select the Bake cycle
4. Close the lid, Turn on the bread maker. Select the White / Basic setting, then select the dough size, select light or medium crust. Press start to start the cycle.
5. When this is done, and the bread is baked, remove the pan from the machine. Let stand a few minutes.
6. Remove the bread from the skillet and leave it on a wire rack to cool for at least 10 minutes. Slice and serve.

168. Perfect Cocoa Bread

Servings: 10
Cooking Time: 3 Hours
Ingredients:
- Milk – 1 cup.
- Egg – 1
- Egg yolk – 1
- Olive oil – 3 tbsps.
- Vanilla extract – 1 tsp.
- Salt – 1 tsp.
- Bread flour – 3 cups.
- Brown sugar – ½ cup.
- Cocoa powder – 1/3 cup.
- Vital wheat gluten – 1 tbsp.
- Yeast – 2 ½ tsps.

Directions:
1. Add all ingredients into the bread machine pan. Select basic setting then select medium crust and start. Once loaf is done, remove the loaf pan from the machine. Allow it to cool for 10 minutes. Slice and serve.

169. Honey Whole-wheat Sandwich Bread

Servings: 14 Slices
Cooking Time: 3 H.
Ingredients:
- 4¼ cups whole-wheat flour
- ½ tsp salt
- 1½ cups water
- ¼ cup honey
- 2 Tbsp olive oil, or melted butter
- 2¼ tsp bread machine yeast (1 packet)

Directions:
1. Add each ingredient to the bread machine in the order and at the temperature recommended by your bread machine manufacturer.
2. Close the lid, select the whole wheat, low crust setting on your bread machine and press start.
3. When the bread machine has finished baking, remove the bread and put it on a cooling rack.

170. Black Forest Loaf

Servings: 1 Loaf
Cooking Time: 3 Hours
Ingredients:
- 1 ½ cups bread flour
- 1 cup whole wheat flour
- 1 cup rye flour
- Three tablespoons cocoa
- One tablespoon caraway seeds
- Two teaspoons yeast
- 1 ½ teaspoons salt
- One ¼ cups water
- 1/3 cup molasses
- 1 ½ tablespoon canola oil

Directions:

1. Combine the ingredients in the bread pan by putting the wet ingredients first, followed by the dry ones.
2. Press the "Normal" or "Basic" mode and light the bread machine's crust colour setting.
3. After the cycles are completed, take out the bread from the machine.
4. Cooldown and then slice the bread.

Nutrition Info: Calories: 136;Carbohydrates: 27g;Fat: 2g;Protein: 3g

171. Anadama Bread

Servings: 2 Loaves
Cooking Time: 45 Minutes
Ingredients:
- 1/2 cup sunflower seeds
- Two teaspoons bread machine yeast
- 4 1/2 cups bread flour
- 3/4 cup yellow cornmeal
- Two tablespoons unsalted butter, cubed
- 1 1/2 teaspoon salt
- 1/4 cup dry skim milk powder
- 1/4 cup molasses
- 1 1/2 cups water, with a temperature of 80 to 90 degrees F (26 to 32 degrees C)

Directions:
1. Put all the pan's ingredients, except the sunflower seeds, in this order: water, molasses, milk, salt, butter, cornmeal, flour, and yeast.
2. Put the pan in the machine and cover the lid.
3. Put the sunflower seeds in the fruit and nut dispenser.
4. Turn the machine on and choose the basic setting and your desired colour of the crust—press start.

Nutrition Info: Calories: 130 calories;Total Carbohydrate: 25 g ;Total Fat: 2 g ;Protein: 3 g

172. Everyday White Bread

Servings: 8 – 16 Slices
Cooking Time: 10 Minutes
Ingredients:
- 8 slice bread (1 pound)
- ¾ cup water, at 80°F to 90°F
- 1 tablespoon melted butter, cooled
- 1 tablespoon sugar
- ¾ teaspoon salt
- 2 tablespoons skim milk powder
- 2 cups white bread flour
- ¾ teaspoon bread machine or instant yeast

Directions:
1. Preparing the Ingredients.
2. Place the ingredients in your bread machine as recommended by the manufacturer.
3. Select the Bake cycle
4. Close the lid, Turn on the bread maker. Select the White / Basic setting, then select the dough size and crust color. Press start to start the cycle.
5. When this is done, and the bread is baked, remove the pan from the machine.
6. Gently shake the bucket to remove the loaf, and turn it out onto a rack to cool.

173. English Muffin Bread

Servings: 1 Loaf
Cooking Time: 10 Minutes
Ingredients:
- 12 slice bread (1½ pounds)
- 1¼ cups buttermilk, at 80°F to 90°F
- 1½ tablespoons melted butter, cooled
- 1½ tablespoons sugar
- 1⅛ teaspoons salt
- ⅓ teaspoon baking powder
- 2⅔ cups white bread flour
- 1⅔ teaspoons bread machine or instant yeast

Directions:
1. Preparing the Ingredients.
2. Place the ingredients in your bread machine as recommended by the manufacturer
3. Select the Bake cycle
4. Close the lid, Turn on the bread maker. Select the White / Basic setting, then select the dough size, select light or medium crust. Press start to start the cycle. When this is done, and the bread is baked, remove the pan from the machine. Let stand a few minutes. Remove the bread from the skillet and leave it on a wire rack to cool for at least 10 minutes. Slice and serve.

174. Italian Restaurant Style Breadsticks

Servings: 12 - 16
Cooking Time: 3 Hours
Ingredients:
- 1 1/2 cups warm water
- 2 tablespoons butter, unsalted and melted
- 4 1/4 cups bread flour
- 2 tablespoons sugar

- 1 tablespoon salt
- 1 package active dry yeast
- For the topping:
- 1 stick unsalted butter, melted
- 2 teaspoons garlic powder
- 1 teaspoons salt
- 1 teaspoon parsley

Directions:
1. Add wet ingredients to your bread maker pan.
2. Mix dry ingredients, except yeast, and add to pan.
3. Make a well in the center of the dry ingredients and add the yeast.
4. Set to Dough cycle and press Start.
5. When the dough is done, roll out and cut into strips; keep in mind that they will double in size after they have risen, so roll them out thinner than a typical breadstick to yield room for them to grow.
6. Place on a greased baking sheet.
7. Cover the dough with a light towel and let sit in a warm area for 45 minutes to an hour.
8. Preheat an oven to 400°F.
9. Bake breadsticks for 6 to 7 minutes.
10. Mix the melted butter, garlic powder, salt and parsley in a small mixing bowl.
11. Brush the bread sticks with half the butter mixture; return to oven and bake for 5 to 8 additional minutes.
12. Remove breadsticks from the oven and brush the other half of the butter mixture.
13. Allow to cool for a few minutes before serving.

Nutrition Info: Calories: 148, Sodium: 450 mg, Dietary Fiber: 1 g, Fat: 2.5 g, Carbs: 27.3 g, Protein: 3.7 g.

175. Almond Flour Bread

Servings: 10 Pcs
Cooking Time: 10 Minutes
Ingredients:
- Four egg whites
- Two egg yolks
- 2 cups almond flour
- 1/4 cup butter, melted
- 2 tbsp psyllium husk powder
- 1 1/2 tbsp baking powder
- 1/2 tsp xanthan gum
- Salt
- 1/2 cup + 2 tbsp warm water
- 2 1/4 tsp yeast

Directions:
1. Use a mixing bowl to combine all of the dry ingredients except for the yeast.
2. In the bread machine pan, add all the wet ingredients.
3. Add all of your dry ingredients from the small mixing bowl to the bread machine pan.
4. Set the machine to the basic setting.
5. When the bread is finished, remove it to the machine pan from the bread machine.
6. Let cool slightly before transferring to a cooling rack.
7. It can be stored for four days on the counter and three months in the freezer.

Nutrition Info: Calories: 110 ;Carbohydrates: 2.4g ;Protein: 4g

176. Banana Lemon Loaf

Servings: 1 Loaf (16 Slices)
Cooking Time: 1 Hour And 30 Minutes
Ingredients:
- 2 cups all-purpose flour
- 1 cup bananas, very ripe and mashed
- 1 cup walnuts, chopped
- 1 cup of sugar
- One tablespoon baking powder
- One teaspoon lemon peel, grated
- ½ teaspoon salt
- Two eggs
- ½ cup of vegetable oil
- Two tablespoons lemon juice

Directions:
1. Put all ingredients into a pan in this order: bananas, wet ingredients, and then dry ingredients.
2. Press the "Quick" or "Cake" setting of your bread machine.
3. Allow the cycles to be completed.
4. Take out the pan from the machine. The cooldown for 10 minutes before slicing the bread enjoy.

Nutrition Info: Calories: 120;Carbohydrates: 15g;Fat: 6g;Protein: 2g

177. Simple White Bread

Servings: 10
Cooking Time: 2 Hours
Ingredients:
- Lukewarm water – 1 ½ cups.
- All-purpose flour – 2 ½ cups.

- Bread flour – 1 cup.
- Baking soda – ¼ tsp.
- Yeast – 2 ½ tsps.
- Olive oil --- 1 tbsp+1 tsp.
- Sugar – 1 ½ tsps.
- Salt – 1 tsp.

Directions:
1. Add all ingredients to the bread machine pan according to the bread machine manufacturer instructions. Select quick bread setting then select medium crust and start. Once the loaf is done, remove the loaf pan from the machine. Allow it to cool for 10 minutes. Slice and serve.

178. Whole Wheat Rolls

Servings: 12
Cooking Time: 3 Hours
Ingredients:
- 1 tablespoon sugar
- 1 teaspoon salt
- 2 3/4 cups whole wheat flour
- 2 teaspoons dry active yeast
- 1/4 cup water
- 1 egg
- 7/8 cup milk
- 1/4 cup butter

Directions:
1. All ingredients should be brought to room temperature before baking.
2. Add the wet ingredients to the bread maker pan.
3. Measure and add the dry ingredients (except yeast) to the pan.
4. Make a well in the center of the dry ingredients and add the yeast.
5. Carefully place the yeast in the hole.
6. Select the Dough cycle, then press Start.
7. Divide dough into 12 portions and shape them into balls.
8. Preheat an oven to 350°F. Place rolls on a greased baking pan.
9. Bake for 25 to 30 minutes, until golden brown.
10. Butter and serve warm.

Nutrition Info: Calories: 147, Sodium: 236 mg, Dietary Fiber: 3.5 g, Fat: 5.1 g, Carbs: 22.1 g, Protein: 5.1 g.

179. 100 Percent Whole-wheat Bread

Servings: 1 Loaf
Cooking Time: 10 Minutes Or Less
Ingredients:
- 12 slice bread (1½ pound)
- 1⅛ cups water, at 80°F to 90°F
- 2¼ tablespoons melted butter, cooled
- 2¼ tablespoons honey
- 1⅛ teaspoons salt
- 3 cups whole-wheat bread flour
- 2 teaspoons sugar
- 2 tablespoons skim milk powder
- ¾ teaspoon salt
- 1½ teaspoons bread machine or instant yeast

Directions:
1. Preparing the Ingredients.
2. Choose the size of bread to prepare. Measure and add the ingredients to the pan in the order as indicated in the ingredient listing. Place the pan in the bread machine and close the lid.
3. Select the Bake cycle
4. Turn on the bread maker. Select the Wheat/Whole setting, then select the dough size and crust color. Press start to start the cycle. When this is done, and the bread is baked, remove the pan from the machine. Let stand a few minutes.
5. Remove the bread from the pan and leave it on a wire rack to cool for at least 10 minutes. Slice and serve.

180. Italian White Bread

Servings: 14 Slices
Cooking Time: 3 H.
Ingredients:
- ¾ cup cold water
- 2 cups bread flour
- 1 Tbsp sugar
- 1 tsp salt
- 1 Tbsp olive oil
- 1 tsp active dry yeast

Directions:
1. Add each ingredient to the bread machine in the order and at the temperature recommended by your bread machine manufacturer.
2. Close the lid, select the Italian or basic bread, low crust setting on your bread machine, and press start.

3. When the bread machine has finished baking, remove the bread and put it on a cooling rack.

181. Classic White Bread I

Servings: 1 Loaf
Cooking Time: 10 Minutes
Ingredients:
- 16 slice bread (2 pounds)
- 1½ cups lukewarm water
- 1 tablespoon + 1 teaspoon olive oil
- 1½ teaspoons sugar
- 1 teaspoon table salt
- ¼ teaspoon baking soda
- 2½ cups all-purpose flour
- 1 cup white bread flour
- 2½ teaspoons bread machine yeast

Directions:
1. Preparing the Ingredients
2. Choose the size of bread to prepare. Measure and add the ingredients to the pan in the order as indicated in the ingredient listing. Place the pan in the bread machine and close the lid.
3. Select the Bake cycle
4. Close the lid, Turn on the bread maker. Select the White / Basic setting, then select the dough size and crust color. Press start to start the cycle.
5. When this is done, and the bread is baked, remove the pan from the machine. Let stand a few minutes.
6. Remove the bread from the pan and leave it on a wire rack to cool for at least 10 minutes.
7. After this time, proceed to cut it

182. Friendship Bread

Servings: 12
Cooking Time: 3 Hours 10 Minutes
Ingredients:
- 1 cup Amish Friendship Bread Starter
- 3 eggs
- 2/3 cup vegetable oil
- 1/4 cup milk
- 1 cup sugar
- 1/2 teaspoon vanilla extract
- 2 teaspoons cinnamon
- 1 1/2 teaspoons baking powder
- 1/2 teaspoon salt
- 1/2 teaspoon baking soda
- 2 cups flour
- 2 small boxes instant vanilla pudding

Directions:
1. Add all of the wet ingredients into the bread maker pan.
2. Add in dry ingredients, except sugar and cinnamon.
3. Set bread machine on Sweet cycle, light crust color and press Start.
4. During the last 30 minutes of baking, lift lid and quickly add 1/4 cup sugar and 1/4 teaspoon of cinnamon.
5. When finished baking, leave in bread machine for 20 minutes to rest.
6. Remove from baking pan and put loaf on a cooling rack.

Nutrition Info: Calories: 379, Sodium: 296 mg, Dietary Fiber: 1.0 g, Fat: 13.7 g, Carbs: 61.25 g, Protein: 5.3 g.

183. Cracked Wheat Bread

Servings: 10
Cooking Time: 1 Hour 20 Minutes
Ingredients:
- 1 1/4 cup plus 1 tablespoon water
- 2 tablespoons vegetable oil
- 3 cups bread flour
- 3/4 cup cracked wheat
- 1 1/2 teaspoons salt
- 2 tablespoons sugar
- 2 1/4 teaspoons active dry yeast

Directions:
1. Bring water to a boil.
2. Place cracked wheat in small mixing bowl, pour water over it and stir.
3. Cool to 80°F.
4. Place cracked wheat mixture into pan, followed by all ingredients (except yeast) in the order listed.
5. Make a well in the center of the dry ingredients and add the yeast.
6. Select the Basic Bread cycle, medium color crust, and press Start.
7. Check dough consistency after 5 minutes of kneading. The dough should be a soft, tacky ball. If it is dry and stiff, add water one 1/2 tablespoon at a time until sticky. If it's too wet and sticky, add 1 tablespoon of flour at a time.
8. Remove bread when cycle is finished and allow to cool before serving.

Nutrition Info: Calories: 232, Sodium: 350 mg, Dietary Fiber: 3.3 g, Fat: 3.3 g, Carbs: 43.7 g, Protein: 6.3 g.

184. Pumpernickel Bread 3

Servings: 12
Cooking Time: 3 Hours 30 Minutes
Ingredients:
- 1 1/4 cups lukewarm water
- 1/4 cup molasses
- 2 tablespoons unsweetened cocoa powder
- 1 teaspoon sea salt
- 1 cup whole wheat flour
- 1 cup rye flour
- 2 cups unbleached all-purpose flour
- 2 1/2 tablespoons vegetable oil
- 1 1/2 tablespoons packed brown sugar
- 1 tablespoon caraway seeds
- 2 1/2 teaspoons instant yeast

Directions:
1. Add all of the ingredients in the order listed above, reserving yeast.
2. Make a well in the center of the dry ingredients and add the yeast.
3. Set the bread maker on Whole Wheat cycle, select crust color, and press Start.
4. Remove and let the loaf cool for 15 minutes before slicing.
5. Note: all ingredients should be at room temperature before baking.

Nutrition Info: Calories: 263, Sodium: 160 mg, Dietary Fiber: 4.7 g, Fat: 3.5 g, Carbs: 50.6 g, Protein: 7.1 g.

185. Mustard Sour Cream Bread

Servings: 1 Loaf
Cooking Time: 1 Hour
Ingredients:
- 1¼ cups (320 ml) lukewarm milk
- Three tablespoons sunflower oil
- Three tablespoons sour cream
- Two tablespoons dry mustard
- One egg
- ½ sachet sugar vanilla
- 4 cups (690 g) wheat flour
- One teaspoon active dry yeast
- Two tablespoons white sugar
- Two teaspoons sea salt

Directions:
1. Prepare all of the ingredients for your bread and measuring means (a cup, a spoon, kitchen scales).
2. Carefully measure the ingredients into the pan.
3. Put all the ingredients into a bread bucket in the right order, follow your manual for the bread machine.
4. Cover it. Select the program of your bread machine to BASIC and choose the crust colour to MEDIUM.
5. Press START. Wait until the program completes.
6. When done, take the bucket out and let it cool for 5-10 minutes.
7. Shake the loaf from the pan and let cool for 30 minutes on a cooling rack.
8. Slice, serve and enjoy the taste of fragrant homemade bread.

Nutrition Info: Calories 340;Total Fat 9.2g;Saturated Fat 1.9g;Cholesterol 26g;Sodium 614mg

186. Golden Raisin Bread

Servings: 1 Loaf
Cooking Time: 10 Minutes
Ingredients:
- 8 slice bread (pounds)
- ¾ cup milk, at 80°F to 90°F
- 1 tablespoon melted butter, cooled
- ¼ cup molasses
- 1 tablespoon sugar
- ¾ teaspoon salt
- 2 cups white bread flour
- 1 teaspoon bread machine or instant yeast
- ½ cup golden raisins
- 12 slice bread (1½ pounds)
- 1⅛ cups milk, at 80°F to 90°F
- 1½ tablespoons melted butter, cooled

Directions:
1. Preparing the Ingredients.
2. Place the ingredients, except the raisins, in your bread machine as recommended by the manufacturer.
3. Select the Bake cycle
4. Program the machine for Basic/White or Sweet bread, select light or medium crust, and press Start. Add the raisins at the raisin/nut signal. When the loaf is done, remove the bucket from the machine.

5. Let the loaf cool for 5 minutes. Gently shake the bucket to remove the loaf, and turn it out onto a rack to cool.

187. Healthy Whole Wheat Bread

Servings: 10
Cooking Time: 2 Hours
Ingredients:
- Water – 1 ½ cups+2 tbsps.
- Vegetable oil – 2 tbsps.
- Salt – 2 tsps.
- Brown sugar – 1/3 cup.
- Whole wheat flour – 4 ¼ cups.
- Milk powder – 3 tbsps.
- Active dry yeast – 2 tsps.

Directions:
1. Add water, oil, salt, brown sugar, whole wheat flour, and milk powder to the bread pan. Make a small hole into the flour with your finger and add yeast to the hole. Make sure yeast will not be mixed with any liquids. Select whole wheat setting then select light/medium crust and start. Once loaf is done, remove the loaf pan from the machine. Allow it to cool for 10 minutes. Slice and serve.

188. Bagels

Servings: 9
Cooking Time: 1 Hour
Ingredients:
- 1 cup warm water
- 1 1/2 teaspoons salt
- 2 tablespoons sugar
- 3 cups bread flour
- 2 1/4 teaspoons active dry yeast
- 3 quarts boiling water
- 3 tablespoons white sugar
- 1 tablespoon cornmeal
- 1 egg white
- Flour, for surface

Directions:
1. Place in the bread machine pan in the following order: warm water, salt, sugar, and flour.
2. Make a well in the center of the dry ingredients and add the yeast.
3. Select Dough cycle and press Start.
4. When Dough cycle is complete, remove pan and let dough rest on a lightly floured surface. Stir 3 tablespoons of sugar into the boiling water.
5. Cut dough into 9 equal pieces and roll each piece into a small ball.
6. Flatten each ball with the palm of your hand. Poke a hole in the middle of each using your thumb. Twirl the dough on your finger to make the hole bigger, while evening out the dough around the hole.
7. Sprinkle an ungreased baking sheet with 1 teaspoon cornmeal. Place the bagel on the baking sheet and repeat until all bagels are formed.
8. Cover the shaped bagels with a clean kitchen towel and let rise for 10 minutes.
9. Preheat an oven to 375°F.
10. Carefully transfer the bagels, one by one, to the boiling water. Boil for 1 minute, turning halfway.
11. Drain on a clean towel. Arrange boiled bagels on the baking sheet.
12. Glaze the tops with egg white and sprinkle any toppings you desire.
13. Bake for 20 to 25 minutes or until golden brown.
14. Let cool on a wire rack before serving.

Nutrition Info: Calories: 185, Sodium: 394 mg, Dietary Fiber: 1.4 g, Fat: 0.5 g, Carbs: 39.7 g, Protein: 5.2 g.

189. Low-carb Multigrain Bread

Servings: 1 Loaf
Cooking Time: 1 Hour And 30 Minutes
Ingredients:
- ¾ cup whole-wheat flour
- ¼ cup cornmeal
- ¼ cup oatmeal
- Two tablespoons 7-grain cereals
- Two tablespoons baking powder
- One teaspoon salt
- ¼ teaspoon baking soda
- ¾ cup of water
- ¼ cup of vegetable oil
- ¼ cup of orange juice
- Three tablespoons aquafaba

Directions:
1. In the bread pan, add the wet ingredients first, then the dry ingredients.
2. Press the "Quick" or "Cake" mode of your bread machine.
3. Wait until all cycles are through.
4. Remove the bread pan from the machine.

5. Let the bread rest for 10 minutes in the pan before taking it out to cool down further.
6. Slice the bread after an hour has passed.
Nutrition Info: Calories: 60;Carbohydrates: 9g;Fat: 2g;Protein: 1g

190. Gluten-free White Bread

Servings: 14 Slices
Cooking Time: 3 H.
Ingredients:
- 2 eggs
- 1⅓ cups milk
- 6 Tbsp oil
- 1 tsp vinegar
- 3⅝ cups white bread flour
- 1 tsp salt
- 2 Tbsp sugar
- 2 tsp dove farm quick yeast

Directions:
1. Add each ingredient to the bread machine in the order and at the temperature recommended by your bread machine manufacturer.
2. Close the lid and start the machine on the gluten free bread program, if available. Alternatively use the basic or rapid setting with a dark crust option.
3. When the bread machine has finished baking, remove the bread and put it on a cooling rack.

191. Mediterranean Semolina Bread

Servings: 1 Loaf (16 Slices)
Cooking Time: 30 Minutes
Ingredients:
- 1 cup lukewarm water (80 degrees F)
- One teaspoon salt
- 2½ tablespoons butter, melted
- 2½ teaspoons white sugar
- 2¼ cups all-purpose flour
- 1/3 cups semolina
- 1½ teaspoons active dry yeast

Directions:
1. Prepare all of the ingredients for your bread and measuring means (a cup, a spoon, kitchen scales).
2. Carefully measure the ingredients into the pan.
3. Put all the ingredients into a bread bucket in the right order. Follow your manual for the bread machine.
4. Close the cover.
5. Select your bread machine's program to ITALIAN BREAD / SANDWICH mode and choose the crust colour to MEDIUM.
6. Press START. Wait until the program completes.
7. When done, take the bucket out and let it cool for 5-10 minutes.
8. Shake the loaf from the pan and let cool for 30 minutes on a cooling rack.
9. Slice and serve.

Nutrition Info: Calories 243;Total Fat 8.1g;Saturated Fat 4.9g;Cholesterol 20g;Sodium 203mg;Total Carbohydrate 37g;Dietary Fiber 1.5g;Total Sugars 2.8g;Protein 5.3g

192. Golden Corn Bread

Servings: 1 Loaf
Cooking Time: 10 Minutes
Ingredients:
- 12 to 16 slices bread (1½ to 2 pounds)
- 1 cup buttermilk, at 80°F to 90°F
- ¼ cup melted butter, cooled
- 2 eggs, at room temperature
- 1⅓ cups all-purpose flour
- 1 cup cornmeal
- ¼ cup sugar
- 2¼ cups whole-wheat bread flour
- 1½ teaspoons bread machine yeast

Directions:
1. Preparing the Ingredients.
2. Place the buttermilk, butter, and eggs in your in your bread machine as recommended by the manufacturer.
3. Select the Bake cycle
4. Program the machine for Quick/Rapid bread and press Start. While the wet ingredients are mixing, stir together the flour, cornmeal, sugar, baking powder, and salt in a small bowl.
5. After the first fast mixing is done and the machine signals, add the dry ingredients. When the loaf is done, remove the bucket from the machine. Let the loaf cool for 5 minutes. Gently shake the bucket to remove the loaf, and turn it out onto a rack to cool.

193. Homemade Wonderful Bread

Servings: 2 Loaves
Cooking Time: 15 Minutes

78

Ingredients:
- 2 1/2 teaspoons active dry yeast
- 1/4 cup warm water
- One tablespoon white sugar
- 4 cups all-purpose flour
- 1/4 cup dry potato flakes
- 1/4 cup dry milk powder
- Two teaspoons salt
- 1/4 cup white sugar
- Two tablespoons margarine
- 1 cup of warm water(45 degrees C)

Directions:
1. Prepare the yeast, 1/4 cup warm water and sugar to whisk and then let it sit in 15 minutes.
2. Take all ingredients together with yeast mixture to put in the pan of bread machine according to the manufacturer's recommended order. Choose basic and light crust settings.

Nutrition Info: Calories: 162 calories;Total Carbohydrate: 31.6 g ;Cholesterol: < 1 mg ;Total Fat: 1.8 g ;Protein: 4.5 g

194. Soft Sandwich Bread

Servings: 14 Slices
Cooking Time: 3 H.
Ingredients:
- 2 Tbsp sugar
- 1 cup water
- 1 Tbsp yeast
- ¼ cup vegetable oil
- 3 cups white flour
- 2 tsp salt

Directions:
1. Add each ingredient to the bread machine in the order and at the temperature recommended by your bread machine manufacturer.
2. Close the lid, select the basic bread, low crust setting on your bread machine and press start.
3. When the bread machine has finished baking, remove the bread and put it on a cooling rack.

195. Multigrain Olive Oil White Bread

Servings: 1 Loaf (16 Slices)
Cooking Time: 1 Hour And 30 Minutes
Ingredients:
- For the Dough
- 300 ml water
- 500 grams bakers flour
- 8 grams dried yeast
- 10 ml salt
- 5 ml caster suger
- 40 ml olive oil
- For the Seed mix
- 40 grams sunflower seeds
- 20 grams sesame seeds
- 20 grams flax seeds
- 20 grams quinoa
- 20 grams pumpkin seeds

Directions:
1. For the water: to 100ml of boiling water add 200ml of cold water.
2. Add the ingredients in the order required by the manufacturer.
3. add the seeds at the time required by your machine.
4. Empty dough onto a floured surface and gently use your finger tips to push some of the air out of it. Shape however you like and place on or in an oiled baking tray. Sprinkle with flour or brush with egg for a glazed finish. Slash the top. Cover and rise for 30 mins.
5. Heat oven to 240C/220C fan/gas 8. Bake for 30-35 mins until browned and crisp.

Nutrition Info: Calories 114.1;Total Fat 3.1 g;Saturated Fat 0.5 g;Polyunsaturated Fat 0.4 g;Monounsaturated Fat 1.9 g;Sodium 83.4 mg;Potassium 0.0 mg;Total Carbohydrate 19.7 g

196. Chocolate Chip Banana Bread

Servings: 1 Loaf
Cooking Time: 10 Minutes
Ingredients:
- Shortening or gluten-free cooking spray, for preparing the pan
- 250 grams All-Purpose Flour Blend
- 1 teaspoon ground cinnamon
- 1 teaspoon xanthan gum
- 1 teaspoon baking powder
- ½ teaspoon baking soda
- ¼ teaspoon salt
- 2 large eggs
- 1 teaspoon vanilla extract
- 90 grams mini semisweet chocolate chips or nondairy alternative
- 80 grams plain Greek yogurt or nondairy alternative

- 450 grams mashed bananas (about 4 large bananas)
- 8 tablespoons (1 stick) butter or nondairy alternative
- 150 grams light brown sugar

Directions:
1. Preparing the Ingredients.
2. Measure and add the ingredients to the pan in the order mentioned above. Place the pan in the bread machine and close the lid.
3. Select the Bake cycle
4. Close the lid, Turn on the bread maker. Select the White / Basic setting, then select the dough size, select light or medium crust. Press start to start the cycle.
5. When this is done, and the bread is baked, remove the pan from the machine. Let the bread cool in the pan for at least 20 minutes, then gently transfer it to a wire rack to cool completely

197. Gluten-free Simple Sandwich Bread

Servings: 1 Loaf
Cooking Time: 10 Minutes
Ingredients:
- 1 1/2 cups sorghum flour
- 1 cup tapioca starch or potato starch (not potato flour)
- 1/2 cup gluten-free millet flour or gluten-free oat flour
- 2 teaspoons xanthan gum
- 1 1/4 teaspoons fine sea salt
- 2 1/2 teaspoons gluten-free yeast for bread machines
- 1 1/4 cups warm water
- 3 tablespoons extra virgin olive oil
- 1 tablespoon honey or raw agave nectar
- 1/2 teaspoon mild rice vinegar or lemon juice
- 2 organic free-range eggs, beaten

Directions:
1. Preparing the Ingredients.
2. Whisk together the dry ingredients except the yeast and set aside.
3. Add the liquid ingredients to the bread maker pan first, then gently pour the mixed dry ingredients on top of the liquid.
4. Make a well in the center of the dry ingredients and add the yeast.
5. Select the Bake cycle

6. Set for Rapid 1 hour 20 minutes, medium crust color, and press Start.
7. Transfer to a cooling rack for 15 minutes before slicing to serve.

198. Slider Buns

Servings: 18
Cooking Time: 3 Hours
Ingredients:
- 1 1/4 cups milk
- 1 egg
- 2 tablespoons butter
- 3/4 teaspoon salt
- 1/4 cup white sugar
- 3 3/4 cups all-purpose flour
- 1 package active dry yeast
- Flour, for surface

Directions:
1. Add all ingredients to the pan of your bread maker in the order listed above.
2. Set bread machine to Dough cycle. Once the Dough cycle is complete, roll dough out on a floured surface to about a 1-inch thickness.
3. Cut out 18 buns with a biscuit cutter or small glass and place them on a greased baking sheet.
4. Let buns rise about one hour or until they have doubled in size.
5. Bake at 350°F for 10 minutes.
6. Brush the tops of baked buns with melted butter and serve.

Nutrition Info: Calories: 130, Sodium: 118 mg, Dietary Fiber: 0.8g, Fat: 2.2 g, Carbs: 23.7 g, Protein: 3.7 g.

199. Beer Bread

Servings: 1 Loaf
Cooking Time: 2.5-3 Hours
Ingredients:
- 3 cups bread flour
- Two tablespoons sugar
- Two ¼ teaspoons yeast
- 1 ½ teaspoons salt
- 2/3 cup beer
- 1/3 cup water
- Two tablespoons vegetable oil

Directions:
1. Add all ingredients into a pan in this order: water, beer, oil, salt, sugar, flour, and yeast.
2. Start the bread machine with the "Basic" or "Normal" mode on and light to medium crust colour.

3. Let the machine complete all cycles.
4. Take out the pan from the machine.
5. Transfer the beer bread into a wire rack to cool it down for about an hour.
6. Cut into 12 slices, and serve.

Nutrition Info: Calories: 130;Carbohydrates: 25g;Fat: 1g;Protein: 4g

200. Rice Flour Rice Bread

Servings: 16 Slices
Cooking Time: 3 H. 15 Min.
Ingredients:
- 3 eggs
- 1½ cups water
- 3 Tbsp vegetable oil
- 1 tsp apple cider vinegar
- 2¼ tsp active dry yeast
- 3¼ cups white rice flour
- 2½ tsp xanthan gum
- 1½ tsp salt
- ½ cup dry milk powder
- 3 Tbsp white sugar

Directions:
1. In a medium-size bowl, mix the eggs, water, oil, and vinegar.
2. In a large bowl, add the yeast, salt, xanthan gum, dry milk powder, rice flour, and sugar. Mix with a whisk until incorporated.
3. Add each ingredient to the bread machine in the order and at the temperature recommended by your bread machine manufacturer.
4. Close the lid, select the whole wheat, medium crust setting on your bread machine, and press start.
5. When the bread machine has finished baking, remove the bread and put it on a cooling rack.

201. Flax Bread

Servings: 8 Pcs
Cooking Time: 18 To 20 Minutes
Ingredients:
- ¾ cup of water
- 200 g ground flax seeds
- ½ cup psyllium husk powder
- 1 Tbsp. baking powder
- Seven large egg whites
- 3 Tbsp. butter
- 2 tsp. salt
- ¼ cup granulated stevia
- One large whole egg
- 1 ½ cups whey protein isolate

Directions:
1. Preheat the oven to 350F.
2. Combine whey protein isolate, psyllium husk, baking powder, sweetener, and salt.
3. In another bowl, mix the water, butter, egg
4. and egg whites.
5. Slowly add psyllium husk mixture to egg mixture and mix well.
6. Grease the pan lightly with butter and pour in the batter.
7. Bake in the oven until the bread is set, about 18 to 20 minutes.

Nutrition Info: Calories: 265.5;Fat: 15.68g;Carb: 1.88g;Protein:24.34 g

202. Dark Rye Bread

Servings: 1 Loaf
Cooking Time: 10 Minutes
Ingredients:
- 12 slice bread (1½ pounds)
- 1 cup water, at 80°F to 90°F
- 1½ tablespoons melted butter, cooled
- 1½ tablespoons unsalted butter, melted
- ⅓ cup molasses
- ⅓ teaspoon salt
- 1½ tablespoons unsweetened cocoa powder
- Pinch ground nutmeg
- ¾ cup rye flour
- 2 cups white bread flour
- 1⅔ teaspoons bread machine or instant yeast

Directions:
1. Preparing the Ingredients.
2. Place the ingredients in your bread machine as recommended by the manufacturer.
3. Select the Bake cycle
4. Turn on the bread maker. Select the White / Basic setting, then select the dough size and crust color. Press start to start the cycle.
5. When this is done, and the bread is baked, remove the pan from the machine. Let stand a few minutes.
6. Remove the bread from the pan and leave it on a wire rack to cool for at least 10 minutes. Slice and serve.

203. Whole Wheat Breakfast Bread

Servings: 14 Slices
Cooking Time: 3 H. 5 Min.
Ingredients:
- 3 cups white whole wheat flour
- ½ tsp salt

81

- 1 cup water
- ½ cup coconut oil, liquified
- 4 Tbsp honey
- 2½ tsp active dry yeast

Directions:
1. Add each ingredient to the bread machine in the order and at the temperature recommended by your bread machine manufacturer.
2. Close the lid, select the basic bread, medium crust setting on your bread machine and press start.
3. When the bread machine has finished baking, remove the bread and put it on a cooling rack.

204. Molasses Wheat Bread

Servings: 1 Loaf
Cooking Time: 10 Minutes Or Less
Ingredients:
- 12 slice bread (1½ pound)
- ¾ cup water, at 80°F to 90°F
- ⅓ cup milk, at 80°F
- 1 tablespoon melted butter, cooled
- 3¾ tablespoons honey
- 2 tablespoons molasses
- 2 teaspoons sugar
- 2 tablespoons skim milk powder
- ¾ teaspoon salt
- 2 teaspoons unsweetened cocoa powder
- 1¾ cups whole-wheat flour
- 1¼ cups white bread flour
- 1⅛ teaspoons bread machine yeast or instant yeast

Directions:
1. Preparing the Ingredients.
2. Choose the size of bread to prepare. Measure and add the ingredients to the pan in the order as indicated in the ingredient listing. Place the pan in the bread machine and close the lid.
3. Select the Bake cycle
4. Turn on the bread maker. Select the White / Basic setting, then select the dough size and crust color. Press start to start the cycle.
5. When this is done, and the bread is baked, remove the pan from the machine. Let stand a few minutes.
6. Remove the bread from the pan and leave it on a wire rack to cool for at least 10 minutes.
7. After this time, proceed to cut it.

205. Peasant Bread

Servings: 12
Cooking Time: 3 Hours
Ingredients:
- 2 tablespoons full rounded yeast
- 2 cups white bread flour
- 1 1/2 tablespoons sugar
- 1 tablespoon salt
- 7/8 cup water
- For the topping:
- Olive oil
- Poppy seeds

Directions:
1. Add water first, then add the dry ingredients to the bread machine, reserving yeast.
2. Make a well in the center of the dry ingredients and add the yeast.
3. Choose French cycle, light crust color, and push Start.
4. When bread is finished, coat the top of loaf with a little olive oil and lightly sprinkle with poppy seeds.
5. Allow to cool slightly and serve warm with extra olive oil for dipping.

Nutrition Info: Calories: 87, Sodium: 583 mg, Dietary Fiber: 1 g, Fat: 0.3 g, Carbs: 18.2 g, Protein: 2.9 g.

206. Mom's White Bread

Servings: 16 Slices
Cooking Time: 3 H.
Ingredients:
- 1 cup and 3 Tbsp water
- 2 Tbsp vegetable oil
- 1½ tsp salt
- 2 Tbsp sugar
- 3¼ cups white bread flour
- 2 tsp active dry yeast

Directions:
1. Add each ingredient to the bread machine in the order and at the temperature recommended by your bread machine manufacturer.
2. Close the lid, select the basic or white bread, medium crust setting on your bread machine, and press start.
3. When the bread machine has finished baking, remove the bread and put it on a cooling rack.

CHEESE & SWEET BREAD

207. Wine And Cheese Bread

Servings: 1 Loaf
Cooking Time: 10 Minutes Plus Fermenting Time
Ingredients:
- 3/4 cup white wine
- 1/2 cup white cheddar or gruyere cheese, shredded
- 1 1/2 tablespoons butter
- 1/2 teaspoon salt
- 3/4 teaspoon sugar
- 2 1/4 cups bread flour
- 1 1/2 teaspoons active dry yeast

Directions:
1. Preparing the Ingredients
2. Add liquid ingredients to the bread maker pan. Add dry ingredients, except yeast, to the bread pan.
3. Use your fingers to form a well-like hole in the flour where you will pour the yeast; yeast must never come into contact with a liquid when you are adding the ingredients. Carefully pour the yeast into the well.
4. Select the Bake cycle
5. Select Basic bread setting, light crust color, and press Start. Allow to cool on a wire rack before serving.

208. Cheese Jalapeno Bread

Servings: 10
Cooking Time: 2 Hours
Ingredients:
- Monterey jack cheese – ¼ cup, shredded
- Active dry yeast – 2 tsps.
- Butter – 1 ½ tbsps.
- Sugar – 1 ½ tbsps.
- Milk – 3 tbsps.
- Flour – 3 cups.
- Water – 1 cup.
- Jalapeno pepper – 1, minced
- Salt – 1 ½ tsps.

Directions:
1. Add all ingredients to the bread machine pan according to the bread machine manufacturer instructions. Select basic bread setting then select light/medium crust and start. Once loaf is done, remove the loaf pan from the machine. Allow it to cool for 10 minutes. Slice and serve.

209. Cocoa Banana Bread

Servings: 1 Loaf
Cooking Time: 10 Minutes Plus Fermenting Time
Ingredients:
- 12 slice bread (1½ pounds)
- 3 bananas, mashed
- 2 eggs, at room temperature
- ¾ cup packed light brown sugar
- ½ cup unsalted butter, melted
- ½ cup sour cream, at room temperature
- ¼ cup sugar
- 1½ teaspoons pure vanilla extract
- 1 cup all-purpose flour
- ½ cup quick oats
- 2 tablespoons unsweetened cocoa powder
- 1 teaspoon baking soda

Directions:
1. Preparing the Ingredients.
2. Choose the size of loaf of your preference and then measure the ingredients.
3. Add all of the ingredients mentioned previously in the list.
4. Close the lid after placing the pan in the bread machine.
5. Select the Bake cycle
6. Turn on the bread machine. Select the Quick/Rapid setting, select the loaf size, and the crust color. Press start.
7. When the cycle is finished, carefully remove the pan from the bread maker and let it rest.
8. Remove the bread from the pan, put in a wire rack to Cool about 5 minutes. Slice

210. Buttery Sweet Bread

Servings: 1 Loaf
Cooking Time: 1 Hour And 15 Minutes
Ingredients:
- 1/3 cup water
- ½ cup milk
- ¼ cup of sugar
- One beaten egg
- One teaspoon of salt
- ¼ cup margarine or ¼ cup butter
- Two teaspoons bread machine yeast

- 3 1/3 cups bread flour

Directions:
1. Put everything in your bread machine pan.
2. Select the white bread setting.
3. Take out the pan when done and set aside for 10 minutes.

Nutrition Info: Calories 168;Carbohydrates: 28g;Total Fat 5g;Cholesterol 0mg;Protein 4g;Fiber 1g;Sugars 3g;Sodium 292mg;Potassium 50mg

211. Apple Butter Bread

Servings: 1 Loaf
Cooking Time: 10 Minutes Plus Fermenting Time
Ingredients:
- 8 slices bread (1 pound)
- ⅔ cup milk, at 80°F to 90°F
- ⅓ cup apple butter, at room temperature
- 4 teaspoons melted butter, cooled
- 2 teaspoons honey
- ⅔ teaspoon salt
- ⅔ cup whole-wheat flour
- 1½ cups white bread flour
- 1 teaspoon bread machine or instant yeast

Directions:
1. Preparing the Ingredients.
2. Choose the size of loaf of your preference and then measure the ingredients.
3. Add all of the ingredients mentioned previously in the list.
4. Close the lid after placing the pan in the bread machine.
5. Select the Bake cycle
6. Turn on the bread machine. Select the Quick/Rapid setting, select the loaf size, and the crust color. Press start.
7. When the cycle is finished, carefully remove the pan from the bread maker and let it rest.
8. Remove the bread from the pan, put in a wire rack to Cool about 5 minutes. Slice

212. Oregano Cheese Bread

Servings: 1 Loaf
Cooking Time: 10 Minutes
Ingredients:
- 3 cups bread flour
- 1 cup water
- ½ cup freshly grated parmesan cheese
- 3 Tbsp sugar
- 1 Tbsp dried leaf oregano
- 1½ Tbsp olive oil
- 1 tsp salt
- 2 tsp active dry yeast

Directions:
1. Preparing the Ingredients
2. Add each ingredient to the bread machine in the order and at the temperature recommended by your bread machine manufacturer.
3. Select the Bake cycle
4. Close the lid, select the basic bread, medium crust setting on your bread machine, and press start.
5. When the bread machine has finished baking, remove the bread and put it on a cooling rack.

213. Crunchy Wheat-and-honey Twist

Servings: 1 Loaf
Cooking Time: 10 Minutes Plus Fermenting Time
Ingredients:
- 16 slice bread (2 pounds)
- Bread dough
- ¾ cup plus 2 tablespoons water
- 2 tablespoons honey
- 1 tablespoon butter, softened
- 1¼ cups whole wheat flour
- 1 cup bread flour
- ⅓ cup slivered almonds, toasted
- 1 teaspoon salt
- 1 teaspoon bread machine or fast-acting dry yeast
- Topping
- Butter, melted
- 1 egg, slightly beaten
- 2 tablespoons sugar
- ¼ teaspoon ground cinnamon

Directions:
1. Preparing the Ingredients.
2. Measure carefully, placing all bread dough ingredients in bread machine pan in the order recommended by the manufacturer.
3. Select Dough/Manual cycle. Do not use delay cycle.
4. Remove dough from pan, using lightly floured hands. Cover and let rest 10 minutes on lightly floured surface.
5. Grease large cookie sheet with shortening. Divide dough in half. Roll each half into 15-inch rope. Place ropes side by side on cookie sheet; twist

together gently and loosely. Pinch ends to seal. Brush melted butter lightly over dough.
6. Select the Bake cycle
7. Cover and let rise in warm place 45 to 60 minutes or until doubled in size.
8. Dough is ready if indentation remains when touched.
9. Heat oven to 375°F. Brush egg over dough. Mix sugar and cinnamon; sprinkle over dough. Bake 25 to 30 minutes or until twist is golden brown and sounds hollow when tapped. Remove from cookie sheet to cooling rack; cool 20 minutes.
10. To toast almonds, bake in ungreased shallow pan at 350°F for 6 to 10 minutes, stirring occasionally, until light brown.

214. Date And Nut Bread

Servings: 1 Loaf
Cooking Time: 2 Hour
Ingredients:
- 1-1/2 tablespoons vegetable oil
- 1 cup of water
- ½ teaspoon salt
- Two tablespoons honey
- ¾ cup whole-wheat flour
- ¾ cup rolled oats
- 1 1/2 teaspoons active dry yeast
- 1 1/2 cups bread flour
- ½ cup almonds, chopped
- ½ cup dates, chopped and pitted

Directions:
1. Put everything in your bread machine pan.
2. Select the primary cycle. Press the start button.
3. Take out the pan when done and set aside for 10 minutes.

Nutrition Info: Calories: 112 Cal;Carbohydrates: 17 g;Fat: 5g;Cholesterol: 0 mg;Protein: 3 g;Fibre: 3 g;Sugar: 7 g;Sodium: 98 mg;Potassium: 130 mg

215. Italian Cheese Bread

Servings: 14 Slices
Cooking Time: 10 Minutes
Ingredients:
- 1¼ cups water
- 3 cups bread flour
- ½ shredded pepper jack cheese
- 2 tsp Italian seasoning
- 2 Tbsp brown sugar
- 1½ tsp salt
- 2 tsp active dry yeast

Directions:
1. Preparing the Ingredients.
2. Add each ingredient to the bread machine in the order and at the temperature recommended by your bread machine manufacturer.
3. Select the Bake cycle
4. Close the lid, select the basic bread, medium crust setting on your bread machine, and press start.
5. When the bread machine has finished baking, remove the bread and put it on a cooling rack.

216. Hot Cross Buns

Servings: 16 Bouns
Cooking Time: 10 Minutes Plus Fermenting Time
Ingredients:
- Dough
- 2 eggs plus enough water to equal 1⅓ cups
- ½ cup butter, softened
- 4 cups bread flour
- ¾ teaspoon ground cinnamon
- ¼ teaspoon ground nutmeg
- 1½ teaspoons salt
- 2 tablespoons granulated sugar
- 1½ teaspoons bread machine or fast-acting dry yeast
- ½ cup raisins
- ½ cup golden raisins
- 1 egg
- 2 tablespoons cold water
- Icing
- 1 cup powdered sugar
- 1 tablespoon milk or water
- ½ teaspoon vanilla

Directions:
1. Preparing the Ingredients.
2. Measure carefully, placing all dough ingredients except raisins, 1 egg and the cold water in bread machine pan in the order recommended by the manufacturer. Add raisins at the Raisin/Nut signal.
3. Select the Bake cycle
4. Select Dough/Manual cycle. Do not use delay cycle. Remove dough from pan, using lightly floured hands. Cover and let rest 10 minutes on lightly floured surface. Grease cookie sheet or 2 (9-inch) round pans. Divide dough in half. Divide each half into 8 equal pieces. Shape each piece into a

smooth ball. Place balls about 2 inches apart on cookie sheet or 1 inch apart in pans. Using scissors, snip a cross shape in top of each ball. Cover and let rise in warm place about 40 minutes or until doubled in size.

5. Heat oven to 375°F. Beat egg and cold water slightly; brush on buns. Bake 18 to 20 minutes or until golden brown. Remove from cookie sheet to cooling rack. Cool slightly.

6. In small bowl, mix all icing ingredients until smooth and spreadable. Make a cross on top of each bun with icing.

217. Delicious Sour Cream Bread

Servings: 1 Loaf
Cooking Time: 10 Minutes Plus Fermenting Time
Ingredients:
- 12 slice bread (1½ pounds)
- ½ cup + 1 tablespoon lukewarm water
- ½ cup + 1 tablespoon sour cream, at room temperature
- 2¼ tablespoons butter, at room temperature
- 1 tablespoon maple syrup
- ¾ teaspoon table salt
- 2¾ cups white bread flour
- 1⅔ teaspoons bread machine yeast

Directions:
1. Preparing the Ingredients.
2. Choose the size of loaf of your preference and then measure the ingredients.
3. Add all of the ingredients mentioned previously in the list.
4. Close the lid after placing the pan in the bread machine.
5. Select the Bake cycle
6. Turn on the bread machine. Select the Basic/White setting, select the loaf size, and the crust color. Press start.
7. When the cycle is finished, carefully remove the pan from the bread maker and let it rest.
8. Remove the bread from the pan, put in a wire rack to Cool about 5 minutes. Slice

218. Parmesan Cheddar Bread

Servings: 1 Loaf
Cooking Time: 10 Minutes Plus Fermenting Time
Ingredients:
- 12 slice bread (1½ pounds)
- 1¼ cups lukewarm milk
- 1 tablespoon unsalted butter, melted
- 2 tablespoons sugar
- 1 teaspoon table salt
- ½ teaspoon freshly ground black pepper
- Pinch cayenne pepper
- 1½ cups shredded aged sharp Cheddar cheese
- ½ cup shredded or grated Parmesan cheese
- 3 cups white bread flour
- 1¼ teaspoons bread machine yeast

Directions:
1. Preparing the Ingredients.
2. Choose the size of loaf of your preference and then measure the ingredients.
3. Add all of the ingredients mentioned previously in the list.
4. Close the lid after placing the pan in the bread machine.
5. Select the Bake cycle
6. Turn on the bread machine. Select the Quick/Rapid setting, select the loaf size, and the crust color. Press start.
7. When the cycle is finished, carefully remove the pan from the bread maker and let it rest.
8. Remove the bread from the pan, put in a wire rack to Cool about 5 minutes. Slice

219. Mozzarella Cheese And Salami Loaf

Servings: 1 Loaf
Cooking Time: 45 Minutes
Ingredients:
- ¾ cup water, set at 80 degrees F
- 1/3 cup mozzarella cheese, shredded
- Four teaspoons sugar
- 2/3 teaspoon salt
- 2/3 teaspoon dried basil
- Pinch of garlic powder
- 2 cups + 2 tablespoons white bread flour
- One teaspoon instant yeast
- ½ cup hot salami, finely diced

Directions:
1. Add the listed ingredients to your bread machine (except salami), following the manufactures instructions.
2. Set the bread machine's program to Basic/White Bread and the crust type to light. Press Start.

3. Let the bread machine work and wait until it beeps. This your indication to add the remaining ingredients at this point, add the salami.
4. Wait until the remaining bake cycle completes.
5. Once the loaf is done, take the bucket out from the bread machine and let it rest for 5 minutes.
6. Gently shake the bucket and remove the loaf, transfer the loaf to a cooling rack and slice.
7. Serve and enjoy!

Nutrition Info: Calories: 164 calories;Total Carbohydrate: 28 g ;Total Fat: 3 g ;Protein: 6 g ;Sugar: 2 g

220. Cinnamon Rum Bread

Servings: 1 Loaf
Ingredients:
- 16 slice bread (2 pounds)
- 1⅛ cups lukewarm water
- 1 egg, at room temperature
- ¼ cup butter, melted and cooled
- ¼ cup sugar
- 4 teaspoons rum extract
- 1⅔ teaspoons table salt
- 4 cups white bread flour
- 1⅓ teaspoons ground cinnamon
- ¼ teaspoon ground nutmeg
- 1⅓ teaspoons bread machine yeast
- 12 slice bread (1½ pounds)
- ¾ cup lukewarm water
- 1 egg, at room temperature
- 3 tablespoons butter, melted and cooled
- 3 tablespoons sugar
- 1 tablespoon rum extract
- 1¼ teaspoons table salt
- 3 cups white bread flour
- 1 teaspoon ground cinnamon
- ¼ teaspoon ground nutmeg
- 1 teaspoon bread machine yeast

Directions:
1. Choose the size of loaf you would like to make and measure your ingredients.
2. Add the ingredients to the bread pan in the order listed above.
3. Place the pan in the bread machine and close the lid.
4. Turn on the bread maker. Select the Sweet setting, then the loaf size, and finally the crust color. Start the cycle.
5. When the cycle is finished and the bread is baked, carefully remove the pan from the machine. Use a potholder as the handle will be very hot. Let rest for a few minutes.
6. Remove the bread from the pan and allow to cool on a wire rack for at least 10 minutes before slicing.

Nutrition Info: (Per Serving):Calories 156, fat 3.7 g, carbs 26.3 g, sodium 248 mg, protein 4.3 g

221. Easy Donuts

Servings: 12
Cooking Time: 1 Hour
Ingredients:
- 2/3 cups milk, room temperature
- 1/4 cup water, room temperature
- ½ cup of warm water
- 1/4 cup softened butter
- One egg slightly has beaten
- 1/4 cup granulated sugar
- 1 tsp salt
- 3 cups bread machine flour
- 2 1/2 tsp bread machine yeast
- oil for deep frying
- 1/4 cup confectioners' sugar

Directions:
1. Place the milk, water, butter, egg sugar, salt, flour, and yeast in a pan.
2. Select dough setting and push start. Press the start button.
3. When the process is complete, remove dough from the pan and transfer it to a lightly floured surface.
4. Using a rolling pin lightly dusted with flour, roll dough to ½ inch thickness.
5. Cut with a floured dusted donut cutter or circle cookie cutter.
6. Transfer donuts to a baking sheet that has been covered with wax paper. Place another layer of paper on top, then cover with a clean tea towel. Let rise 30-40 minutes.
7. Heat vegetable oil to 375º (190ºCº) in a deep-fryer or large, heavy pot.
8. Fry donuts 2-3 at a time until golden brown on both sides for about 3 minutes.
9. Drain on a paper towel.
10. Sprinkle with confectioners' sugar.

Nutrition Info: Calories 180;Carbohydrates: 30g;Total Fat 5g;Cholesterol 25mg;Protein

4g;Fiber 2g;Sugar 7g;Sodium 240mg;Potassium 64mg

222. Prosciutto Parmesan Breadsticks

Servings: 12
Cooking Time: 10 Minutes
Ingredients:
- 1 1/3 cups warm water
- 1 tablespoon butter
- 1 1/2 tablespoons sugar
- 1 1/2 teaspoons salt
- 4 cups bread flour
- 2 teaspoons yeast
- For the topping:
- 1/2 pound prosciutto, sliced very thin
- 1/2 cup of grated parmesan cheese
- 1 egg yolk
- 1 tablespoon of water

Directions:
1. Preparing the Ingredients
2. Place the first set of dough ingredients (except yeast) in the bread pan in the order indicated. Do not add any of the topping ingredients yet. Make a well in the center of the dry ingredients and add the yeast.
3. Select the Bake cycle
4. Select the Dough cycle on the bread machine. When finished, drop the dough onto a lightly-floured surface.
5. Roll the dough out flat to about 1/4-inch thick, or about half a centimeter. Cover with plastic wrap and let rise for 20 to 30 minutes.
6. Sprinkle dough evenly with parmesan and carefully lay the prosciutto slices on the surface of the dough to cover as much of it as possible. Preheat an oven to 400°F.
7. Cut the dough into 12 long strips, about one inch wide. Twist each end in opposite directions, twisting the toppings into the bread stick. Place the breadsticks onto a lightly greased baking sheet. Whisk the egg yolk and water together in a small mixing bowl and lightly baste each breadstick. Bake for 8 to 10 minutes or until golden brown.
8. Remove from oven and serve warm.

223. Parsley Garlic Bread

Servings: 1 Loaf
Cooking Time: 10 Minutes
Ingredients:
- 12 slice bread (1½ pounds)
- 1 cup lukewarm milk
- 1½ tablespoons unsalted butter, melted
- 1 tablespoon sugar
- 1½ teaspoons table salt
- 2 teaspoons garlic powder
- 2 teaspoons fresh parsley, chopped
- 3 cups white bread flour
- 1¾ teaspoons bread machine yeast

Directions:
1. Preparing the Ingredients.
2. Choose the size of loaf of your preference and then measure the ingredients.
3. Add all of the ingredients mentioned previously in the list.
4. Close the lid after placing the pan in the bread machine.
5. Select the Bake cycle
6. Turn on the bread machine. Select the White/Basic setting, select the loaf size, and the crust color. Press start.
7. When the cycle is finished, carefully remove the pan from the bread maker and let it rest.
8. Remove the bread from the pan, put in a wire rack to Cool about 10 minutes. Slice

224. Allspice Currant Bread

Servings: 1 Loaf
Ingredients:
- 16 slice bread (2 pounds)
- 1½ cups lukewarm water
- 2 tablespoons unsalted butter, melted
- ¼ cup sugar
- ¼ cup skim milk powder
- 2 teaspoons table salt
- 4 cups white bread flour
- 1½ teaspoons dried lemon zest
- ¾ teaspoon ground allspice
- ¼ teaspoon ground nutmeg
- 2½ teaspoons bread machine yeast
- 1 cup dried currants
- 12 slice bread (1½ pounds)
- 1⅛ cups lukewarm water
- 1½ tablespoons unsalted butter, melted
- 3 tablespoons sugar
- 3 tablespoons skim milk powder

- 1½ teaspoons table salt
- 3 cups white bread flour
- 1 teaspoon dried lemon zest
- ½ teaspoon ground allspice
- ¼ teaspoon ground nutmeg
- 2½ teaspoons bread machine yeast
- ¾ cup dried currants

Directions:
1. Choose the size of loaf you would like to make and measure your ingredients.
2. Add all of the ingredients except for the dried currants to the bread pan in the order listed above.
3. Place the pan in the bread machine and close the lid.
4. Turn on the bread maker. Select the White/Basic or Fruit/Nut (if your machine has this setting) setting, then the loaf size, and finally the crust color. Start the cycle.
5. When the machine signals to add ingredients, add the dried currants. (Some machines have a fruit/nut hopper where you can add the dried currants when you start the machine. The machine will automatically add them to the dough during the baking process.)
6. When the cycle is finished and the bread is baked, carefully remove the pan from the machine. Use a potholder as the handle will be very hot. Let rest for a few minutes.
7. Remove the bread from the pan and allow to cool on a wire rack for at least 10 minutes before slicing.

Nutrition Info: (Per Serving):Calories 168, fat 2.5 g, carbs 32.3 g, sodium 306 mg, protein 4.8 g

225. Savory Cheddar Cheese Bread

Servings: 16
Cooking Time: 3 Hours And 25 Minutes
Ingredients:
- Lukewarm milk – 1 cup
- All-purpose flour – 3 cups
- Salt - 1 ¼ tsp.
- Sugar – 1 tbsp.
- Grated cheddar cheese – 1 cup
- Cheese powder – ¼ cup
- Instant yeast – 1 ½ tsp.
- Tabasco sauce – ½ tsp.

Directions:
1. Add everything in the bread machine according to bread machine recommendations.
2. Select Basic cycle and Light crust.
3. Remove the bread when finished.
4. Cool, slice, and serve.

Nutrition Info: (Per Serving): Calories: 130; Total Fat: 3.5 g; Saturated Fat: 2 g; Carbohydrates: 19 g; Cholesterol: 10 mg; Fiber: 1 g; Calcium: 37 mg; Sodium: 320 mg; Protein: 5 g

226. Cashew Butter/peanut Butter Bread

Servings: 1 Loaf
Cooking Time: 10 Minutes Plus Fermenting Time
Ingredients:
- 12 slice bread (1½ pounds)
- 1 cup peanut butter or cashew butter
- 1 cup lukewarm milk
- ½ cup packed light brown sugar
- ¼ cup sugar
- ¼ cup butter, at room temperature
- 1 egg, at room temperature
- 2 teaspoons pure vanilla extract
- 2 cups all-purpose flour
- 1 tablespoon baking powder
- ½ teaspoon table salt

Directions:
1. Preparing the Ingredients.
2. Choose the size of loaf of your preference and then measure the ingredients. Add all of the ingredients mentioned previously in the list. Close the lid after placing the pan in the bread machine.
3. Select the Bake cycle
4. Turn on the bread machine. Select the Quick/Rapid setting, select the loaf size, and the crust color. Press start.
5. When the cycle is finished, carefully remove the pan from the bread maker and let it rest.
6. Remove the bread from the pan, put in a wire rack to Cool about 5 minutes. Slice

227. Ricotta Bread

Servings: 14 Slices
Cooking Time: 3 H. 15 Min.
Ingredients:
- 3 Tbsp skim milk
- ⅔ cup ricotta cheese
- 4 tsp unsalted butter, softened to room temperature
- 1 large egg
- 2 Tbsp granulated sugar

- ½ tsp salt
- 1½ cups bread flour, + more flour, as needed
- 1 tsp active dry yeast

Directions:
1. Add each ingredient to the bread machine in the order and at the temperature recommended by your bread machine manufacturer.
2. Close the lid, select the basic bread, medium crust setting on your bread machine, and press start.
3. When the bread machine has finished baking, remove the bread and put it on a cooling rack.

228. Chocolate Orange Bread

Servings: 14 Slices
Cooking Time: 10 Minutes Plus Fermenting Time
Ingredients:
- 1⅝ cups strong white bread flour
- 2 Tbsp cocoa
- 1 tsp ground mixed spice
- 1 egg, beaten
- ½ cup water
- ¼ cup orange juice
- 2 Tbsp butter
- 3 Tbsp light muscovado sugar
- 1 tsp salt
- 1½ tsp easy bake yeast
- ¾ cup mixed peel
- ¾ cup chocolate chips

Directions:
1. Preparing the Ingredients
2. Sift the flour, cocoa, and spices together in a bowl.
3. Add each ingredient to the bread machine in the order and at the temperature recommended by your bread machine manufacturer.
4. Select the Bake cycle
5. Close the lid, select the sweet loaf, medium crust setting on your bread machine, and press start.
6. Add the mixed peel and chocolate chips 5 to 10 minutes before the last kneading cycle ends.
7. When the bread machine has finished baking, remove the bread and put it on a cooling rack.

229. Cheesy Chipotle Bread

Servings: 1 Loaf
Cooking Time: 10 Minutes
Ingredients:
- 8 slice bread (1 pounds)
- ⅔ cup water, at 80°F to 90°F
- 1½ tablespoons sugar
- 1½ tablespoons powdered skim milk
- ¾ teaspoon salt
- ½ teaspoon chipotle chili powder
- 2 cups white bread flour
- ½ cup (2 ounces) shredded sharp Cheddar cheese
- ¾ teaspoon bread machine or instant yeast

Directions:
1. Preparing the Ingredients.
2. Choose the size of loaf of your preference and then measure the ingredients.
3. Add all of the ingredients mentioned previously in the list.
4. Close the lid after placing the pan in the bread machine.
5. Select the Bake cycle
6. Turn on the bread machine. Select the White/Basic setting, select the loaf size, and the crust color. Press start.
7. When the cycle is finished, carefully remove the pan from the bread maker and let it rest.
8. Remove the bread from the pan, put in a wire rack to Cool about 5 minutes. Slice

230. Chocolate Chip Peanut Butter Banana Bread

Servings: 1 Loaf
Cooking Time: 10 Minutes Plus Fermenting Time
Ingredients:
- 12 to 16 slice bread (1½ to 2 pounds)
- 2 bananas, mashed
- 2 eggs, at room temperature
- ½ cup melted butter, cooled
- 2 tablespoons milk, at room temperature
- 1 teaspoon pure vanilla extract
- 2 cups all-purpose flour
- ½ cup sugar
- 1¼ teaspoons baking powder
- ½ teaspoon baking soda
- ½ teaspoon salt
- ½ cup peanut butter chips
- ½ cup semisweet chocolate chips

Directions:
1. Preparing the Ingredients.

2. Stir together the bananas, eggs, butter, milk, and vanilla in the bread machine bucket and set it aside.
3. In a medium bowl, toss together the flour, sugar, baking powder, baking soda, salt, peanut butter chips, and chocolate chips.
4. Add the dry ingredients to the bucket.
5. Select the Bake cycle
6. Program the machine for Quick/Rapid bread, and press Start.
7. When the loaf is done, stick a knife into it, and if it comes out clean, the loaf is done.
8. If the loaf needs a few more minutes, check the control panel for a Bake Only button and extend the time by 10 minutes.
9. When the loaf is done, remove the bucket from the machine. Let the loaf cool for 5 minutes.
10. Gently shake the bucket to remove the loaf, and turn it out onto a rack to cool.

231. Italian Herb Cheese Bread

Servings: 10
Cooking Time: 3 Hours
Ingredients:
- Yeast – 1 ½ tsps.
- Italian herb seasoning – 1 tbsp.
- Brown sugar – 2 tbsps.
- Cheddar cheese – 1 cup., shredded
- Bread flour – 3 cups.
- Butter – 4 tbsps.
- Warm milk – 1 ¼ cups.
- Salt – 2 tsps.

Directions:
1. Add milk into the bread pan. Add remaining ingredients except for yeast to the bread pan. Make a small hole into the flour with your finger and add yeast to the hole. Make sure yeast will not be mixed with any liquids. Select basic setting then select light crust and start. Once loaf is done, remove the loaf pan from the machine. Allow it to cool for 10 minutes. Slice and serve.

232. Cottage Cheese And Chive Bread

Servings: 14 Servings
Cooking Time: 10 Minutes
Ingredients:
- ⅜ cup water
- 1 cup cottage cheese
- 1 large egg
- 2 Tbsp butter
- 1½ tsp salt
- 3¾ cups white bread flour
- 3 Tbsp dried chives
- 2½ Tbsp granulated sugar
- 2¼ tsp active dry yeast

Directions:
1. Preparing the Ingredients
2. Add each ingredient to the bread machine in the order and at the temperature recommended by your bread machine manufacturer.
3. Select the Bake cycle
4. Close the lid, select the basic bread, medium crust setting on your bread machine, and press start.
5. When the bread machine has finished baking, remove the bread and put it on a cooling rack.

233. Sugared Doughnuts

Servings: 20 Doughnuts
Cooking Time: 30 Minutes Plus Fermenting Time
Ingredients:
- ⅔ cup milk
- ¼ cup water
- ¼ cup butter, softened
- 1 egg
- 3 cups bread flour
- ¼ cup sugar
- 1 teaspoon salt
- 2½ teaspoons bread machine or fast-acting dry yeast
- Vegetable oil
- Additional sugar, if desired

Directions:
1. Preparing the Ingredients.
2. Choose the size of loaf of your preference and then measure the ingredients.
3. Add all of the ingredients mentioned previously in the list, except for the vegetable oil and additional sugar. Close the lid after placing the pan in the bread machine.
4. Select the Bake cycle
5. Select Dough/Manual cycle. Do not use delay cycle. Remove dough from pan, using lightly floured hands. Cover and let rest 10 minutes on lightly floured board. Roll dough to ⅜-inch thickness on lightly floured board. Cut with floured

doughnut cutter. Cover and let rise on board 35 to 45 minutes or until slightly raised.
6. In deep fryer or heavy Dutch oven, heat 2 to 3 inches oil to 375°F. Fry doughnuts in oil, 2 or 3 at a time, turning as they rise to the surface. Fry 2 to 3 minutes or until golden brown on both sides. Remove from oil with slotted spoon to cooling rack. Roll warm doughnuts in sugar.

234. Parmesan Tomato Basil Bread

Servings: 10
Cooking Time: 2 Hours
Ingredients:
- Sun-dried tomatoes – ¼ cup, chopped
- Yeast – 2 tsps.
- Bread flour – 2 cups.
- Parmesan cheese – 1/3 cup, grated
- Dried basil – 2 tsps.
- Sugar – 1 tsp.
- Olive oil – 2 tbsps.
- Milk – ¼ cup.
- Water – ½ cup.
- Salt – 1 tsp.

Directions:
1. Add all ingredients except for sun-dried tomatoes into the bread machine pan. Select basic setting then select medium crust and press start. Add sun-dried tomatoes just before the final kneading cycle. Once loaf is done, remove the loaf pan from the machine. Allow it to cool for 10 minutes. Slice and serve.

235. Cream Cheese Bread

Servings: 1 Loaf
Cooking Time: 35 Minutes
Ingredients:
- 1/2 cup Water
- 1/2 cup Cream cheese, softened
- Two tablespoons melted butter
- 1 Beaten egg
- Four tablespoons Sugar
- One teaspoon salt
- 3 cups bread flour
- 1 1/2 teaspoons Active dry yeast

Directions:
1. Place the ingredients in the pan in order, as suggested by your bread machine.
2. After removing it from a machine, place it in a greased 9x5 loaf pan after the cycle.

3. Cover and let rise until doubled.
4. Bake in a 350° oven for approximately 35 minutes.
Nutrition Info: Calories: 150 calories;Total Carbohydrate: 24 g ;Total Fat: 5 g ;Protein: 3 g

236. Hawaiian Sweet Bread

Servings: 1 Loaf
Cooking Time: 2 Hour
Ingredients:
- 3/4 cup pineapple juice
- One egg
- Two tablespoons vegetable oil
- 2 1/2 tablespoons honey
- 3/4 teaspoon salt
- 3 cups bread flour
- Two tablespoons dry milk
- Two teaspoons fast-rising yeast

Directions:
1. Place ingredients in bread machine container.
2. Select the white bread cycle.
3. Press the start button.
4. Take out the pan when done and set aside for 10 minutes.
Nutrition Info: Calories 169;Carbohydrates: 25g;Total Fat 5g;Cholesterol 25mg;Protein 4g;Fiber 1g;Sugar 5g;Sodium 165mg;Potassium 76mg

237. Delicious Italian Cheese Bread

Servings: 10
Cooking Time: 2 Hours
Ingredients:
- Active dry yeast – 2 tsps.
- Brown sugar – 2 tbsps.
- Parmesan cheese – 2 tbsps., grated
- Ground black pepper – 1 tsp.
- Italian seasoning – 2 tsps.
- Pepper jack cheese – 1/2 cup., shredded
- Bread flour – 3 cups.
- Warm water – 1 ¼ cups
- Salt – 1 ½ tsps.

Directions:
1. Add all ingredients into the bread machine pan. Select basic setting then select light/medium crust and start. Once loaf is done, remove the loaf pan from the machine. Allow it to cool for 10 minutes. Slice and serve.

238. Cinnamon Cranberry Bread

Servings: 10
Cooking Time: 3 Hours
Ingredients:
- Water – 1 ¼ cups.
- Butter – 2 tbsps.
- Sugar – 2 ½ tbsps.
- Bread flour – 3 ½ cups.
- Dry yeast – 2 ¼ tsps.
- Dried cranberries – 1 cup.
- Cinnamon – 1 ½ tsps.
- Salt – 1 tsp.

Directions:
1. Add all ingredients except for cranberries and cinnamon into the bread machine pan. Select basic setting then select light crust and press start. Add cranberries and cinnamon just before the final kneading cycle. Once loaf is done, remove the loaf pan from the machine. Allow it to cool for 10 minutes. Slice and serve.

239. Blue Cheese Bread

Servings: 12 Slices
Cooking Time: 10 Minutes
Ingredients:
- 3/4 cup warm water
- 1 large egg
- 1 teaspoon salt
- 3 cups bread flour
- 1 cup blue cheese, crumbled
- 2 tablespoons nonfat dry milk
- 2 tablespoons sugar
- 1 teaspoon bread machine yeast

Directions:
1. Preparing the Ingredients
2. Add the ingredients to bread machine pan in the order listed above, (except yeast) ; be sure to add the cheese with the flour.
3. Make a well in the flour; pour the yeast into the hole.
4. Select the Bake cycle
5. Select Basic bread cycle, medium crust color, and press Start.
6. When finished, transfer to a cooling rack for 10 minutes and serve warm.

240. Jalapeño Corn Bread

Servings: 1 Loaf
Cooking Time: 10 Minutes
Ingredients:
- 12 to 16 slices bread (1½ to 2 pounds)
- 1 cup buttermilk, at 80°F to 90°F
- ¼ cup melted butter, cooled
- 2 eggs, at room temperature
- 1 jalapeño pepper, chopped
- 1⅓ cups all-purpose flour
- 1 cup cornmeal
- ½ cup (2 ounces) shredded Cheddar cheese
- ¼ cup sugar
- 1 tablespoon baking powder
- ½ teaspoon salt

Directions:
1. Preparing the Ingredients.
2. Choose the size of loaf of your preference and then measure the ingredients.
3. Add all of the ingredients mentioned previously in the list.
4. Close the lid after placing the pan in the bread machine.
5. Select the Bake cycle
6. Turn on the bread machine. Select the Quick/Rapid setting, select the loaf size, and the crust color. Press start.
7. When the cycle is finished, carefully remove the pan from the bread maker and let it rest.
8. Remove the bread from the pan, put in a wire rack to Cool about 5 minutes. Slice

241. Apricot–cream Cheese Ring

Servings: 10 Servings
Cooking Time: 10 Minutes
Ingredients:
- ⅓ cup water
- 2 tablespoons butter, softened
- 1 egg
- 2 cups bread flour
- 2 tablespoons sugar
- ½ teaspoon salt
- 1¾ teaspoons bread machine or fast-acting dry yeast
- filling
- 1 package (3 oz) cream cheese, softened
- 1½ tablespoons bread flour
- ¼ cup apricot preserves
- 1 egg, beaten
- 2 tablespoons sliced almonds

Directions:

93

1. Preparing the Ingredients.
2. Measure carefully, placing all bread dough ingredients in bread machine pan in the order recommended by the manufacturer.
3. Select Dough/Manual cycle. Do not use delay cycle.
4. Remove dough from pan, using lightly floured hands. Cover and let rest 10 minutes on lightly floured surface. In small bowl, mix cream cheese and 1½ tablespoons flour.
5. 4 Grease 9-inch round pan with shortening. Roll dough into 15-inch round.
6. Place in pan, letting side of dough hang over edge of pan. Spread cream cheese mixture over dough in pan; spoon apricot preserves onto cream cheese mixture.
7. Select the Bake cycle
8. Make cuts along edge of dough at 1-inch intervals to about ½ inch above cream cheese mixture. Twist pairs of dough strips and fold over cream cheese mixture.
9. Cover and let rise in warm place 40 to 50 minutes or until almost double.
10. 5 Heat oven to 375°F. Brush beaten egg over dough. Sprinkle with almonds.
11. Bake 30 to 35 minutes or until golden brown. Cool at least 30 minutes before cutting.

242. Romano Oregano Bread

Servings: 1 Loaf
Ingredients:
- 16 slice bread (2 pounds)
- 1⅓ cups lukewarm water
- ¼ cup sugar
- 2 tablespoons olive oil
- 1⅓ teaspoons table salt
- 1⅓ tablespoons dried leaf oregano
- ⅔ cup cheese (Romano or Parmesan), freshly grated
- 4 cups white bread flour
- 2½–3 teaspoons bread machine yeast
- 12 slice bread (1½ pounds)
- 1 cup lukewarm water
- 3 tablespoons sugar
- 1½ tablespoons olive oil
- 1 teaspoon table salt
- 1 tablespoon dried leaf oregano
- ½ cup cheese (Romano or Parmesan), freshly grated
- 3 cups white bread flour
- 2 teaspoons bread machine yeast

Directions:
1. Choose the size of loaf you would like to make and measure your ingredients.
2. Add the ingredients to the bread pan in the order listed above.
3. Place the pan in the bread machine and close the lid.
4. Turn on the bread maker. Select the White/Basic setting, then the loaf size, and finally the crust color. Start the cycle.
5. When the cycle is finished and the bread is baked, carefully remove the pan from the machine. Use a potholder as the handle will be very hot. Let rest for a few minutes.
6. Remove the bread from the pan and allow to cool down on a wire rack for at least 10 minutes or more before slicing.

Nutrition Info: (Per Serving):Calories 207, fat 6.2 g, carbs 27 g, sodium 267 mg, protein 9.3 g

243. Garlic Parmesan Bread

Servings: 10
Cooking Time: 3 Hours 45 Minutes
Ingredients:
- Active dry yeast – ¼ oz.
- Sugar – 3 tbsps.
- Kosher salt – 2 tsps.
- Dried oregano – 1 tsp.
- Dried basil – 1 tsp.
- Garlic powder – ½ tsp.
- Parmesan cheese – ½ cup, grated
- All-purpose flour – 3 ½ cups
- Garlic – 1 tbsp., minced
- Butter – ¼ cup, melted
- Olive oil – 1/3 cup
- Water – 1 1/3 cups

Directions:
1. Add water, oil, butter, and garlic into the bread pan. Add remaining ingredients except for yeast to the bread pan. Make a small hole in the flour with your finger and add yeast to the hole. Make sure yeast will not be mixed with any liquids. Select basic setting then select light crust and start. Once loaf is done, remove the loaf pan from the machine. Allow it to cool for 10 minutes. Slice and serve.

244. Choco Chip Pumpkin Bread

Servings: 10
Cooking Time: 2 Hours
Ingredients:
- Eggs – 2
- Chocolate chips – 1/3 cup.
- Brown sugar – 1 ½ cups.
- Vegetable oil – ½ cup.
- Can pumpkin puree – 15 oz.
- Baking powder – 1 tsp.
- Baking soda – 1 tsp.
- Cinnamon – 1 tsp.
- Pumpkin pie spice – 2 tsps.
- All-purpose flour – 2 cups.
- Salt – ½ tsp.

Directions:
1. Add all ingredients except for chocolate chips into the bread machine pan. Select quick bread setting then select light crust and press start. Add chocolate chips just before the final kneading cycle. Once loaf is done, remove the loaf pan from the machine. Allow it to cool for 10 minutes. Slice and serve.

245. Onion, Garlic, Cheese Bread

Servings: 1 Loaf
Cooking Time: 40 Minutes
Ingredients:
- Three tablespoons dried minced onion
- 3 cups bread flour
- Two teaspoons Garlic powder
- Two teaspoons Active dry yeast
- Two tablespoons White sugar
- Two tablespoons Margarine
- Two tablespoons Dry milk powder
- 1 cup shredded sharp cheddar cheese
- 1 1/8 cups warm water
- 1 1/2 teaspoon salt

Directions:
1. In the order suggested by the manufacturer, put the flour, water, powdered milk, margarine or butter, salt, and yeast in the bread pan.
2. Press the basic cycle with a light crust. When the manufacturer directs the sound alerts, add two teaspoons of the onion flakes, the garlic powder, and shredded cheese.
3. After the last kneed, sprinkle the remaining onion flakes over the dough.

Nutrition Info: Calories: 204 calories;Total Carbohydrate: 29 g ;Total Fat: 6 g ;Protein: 8 g

246. Cinnamon Bread

Servings: 1 Loaf
Cooking Time: 10 Minutes Plus Fermenting Time
Ingredients:
- 12 slice bread (1½ pounds)
- ¾ cup lukewarm water
- 1 egg, at room temperature
- 3 tablespoons butter, melted and cooled
- 3 tablespoons sugar
- 1 tablespoon rum extract
- 1¼ teaspoons table salt
- 3 cups white bread flour
- 1 teaspoon ground cinnamon
- ¼ teaspoon ground nutmeg
- 1 teaspoon bread machine yeast

Directions:
1. Preparing the Ingredients.
2. Choose the size of loaf of your preference and then measure the ingredients.
3. Add all of the ingredients mentioned previously in the list.
4. Close the lid after placing the pan in the bread machine.
5. Select the Bake cycle
6. Turn on the bread machine. Select the Basic/White setting, select the loaf size, and the crust color. Press start.
7. When the cycle is finished, carefully remove the pan from the bread maker and let it rest.
8. Remove the bread from the pan, put in a wire rack to Cool about 5 minutes. Slice

247. Chocolate Oatmeal Banana Bread

Servings: 1 Loaf
Cooking Time: 10 Minutes Plus Fermenting Time
Ingredients:
- 12 to 16 slice bread (1½ to 2 pounds)
- 3 bananas, mashed
- 2 eggs, at room temperature
- ¾ cup packed light brown sugar
- ½ cup (1 stick) butter, at room temperature
- ½ cup sour cream, at room temperature
- ¼ cup sugar
- 1½ teaspoons pure vanilla extract

- 1 cup all-purpose flour
- ½ cup quick oats
- 2 tablespoons unsweetened cocoa powder
- 1 teaspoon baking soda

Directions:
1. Preparing the Ingredients.
2. Place the banana, eggs, brown sugar, butter, sour cream, sugar, and vanilla in your bread machine.
3. Program the machine for Quick/Rapid bread and press Start.
4. While the wet ingredients are mixing, stir together the flour, oats, cocoa powder, and baking soda in a small bowl.
5. Select the Bake cycle
6. After the first fast mixing is done and the machine signals, add the dry ingredients.
7. When the loaf is done, remove the bucket from the machine.
8. Let the loaf cool for 5 minutes.
9. Gently shake the bucket to remove the loaf, and turn it out onto a rack to cool.

248. Milk Sweet Bread

Servings: 1 Loaf
Ingredients:
- 16 slice bread (2 pounds)
- 1⅓ cups lukewarm milk
- 1 egg, at room temperature
- 2⅔ tablespoons butter, softened
- ⅔ cup sugar
- 1⅓ teaspoons table salt
- 4 cups white bread flour
- 2¼ teaspoons bread machine yeast
- 12 slice bread (1½ pounds)
- 1 cup lukewarm milk
- 1 egg, at room temperature
- 2 tablespoons butter, softened
- ½ cup sugar
- 1 teaspoon table salt
- 3 cups white bread flour
- 2¼ teaspoons bread machine yeast

Directions:
1. Choose the size of loaf you would like to make and measure your ingredients.
2. Add the ingredients to the bread pan in the order listed above.
3. Place the pan in the bread machine and close the lid.
4. Turn on the bread maker. Select the Sweet setting, then the loaf size, and finally the crust color. Start the cycle.
5. When the cycle is finished and the bread is baked, carefully remove the pan from the machine. Use a potholder as the handle will be very hot. Let rest for a few minutes.
6. Remove the bread from the pan and allow to cool on a wire rack for at least 10 minutes before slicing.

Nutrition Info: (Per Serving):Calories 178, fat 3.2 g, carbs 32.6 g, sodium 227 mg, protein 4.8 g

249. Olive And Cheddar Loaf

Servings: 1 Loaf
Cooking Time: 45 Minutes
Ingredients:
- 1 cup water, room temperature
- Four teaspoons sugar
- ¾ teaspoon salt
- 1 and 1/ cups sharp cheddar cheese, shredded
- 3 cups bread flour
- Two teaspoons active dry yeast
- ¾ cup pimiento olives, drained and sliced

Directions:
1. Add the listed ingredients to your bread machine (except salami), following the manufactures instructions.
2. Set the bread machine's program to Basic/White Bread and the crust type to light. Press Start.
3. Let the bread machine work and wait until it beeps this your indication to add the remaining ingredients. At this point, add the salami.
4. Wait until the remaining bake cycle completes.
5. Once the loaf is done, take the bucket out from the bread machine and let it rest for 5 minutes.
6. Gently shake the bucket and remove the loaf, transfer the loaf to a cooling rack and slice.
7. Serve and enjoy!

Nutrition Info: Calories: 124 calories;Total Carbohydrate: 19 g ;Total Fat: 4 g ;Protein: 5 g ;Sugar: 5 g

250. Crusty Honey Bread

Servings: 1 Loaf
Cooking Time: 10 Minutes Plus Fermenting Time
Ingredients:
- 12 slice bread (1½ pounds)

- 1 cup minus 1 tablespoon water, at 80°F to 90°F
- 1½ tablespoons honey
- 1⅛ tablespoons melted butter, cooled
- ¾ teaspoon salt
- 2⅔ cups white bread flour
- 1½ teaspoons bread machine or instant yeast

Directions:
1. Preparing the Ingredients.
2. Choose the size of loaf of your preference and then measure the ingredients.
3. Add all of the ingredients mentioned previously in the list.
4. Close the lid after placing the pan in the bread machine.
5. Select the Bake cycle
6. Turn on the bread machine. Select the Basic/White setting, select the loaf size, and the crust color. Press start.
7. When the cycle is finished, carefully remove the pan from the bread maker and let it rest.
8. Remove the bread from the pan, put in a wire rack to Cool about 5 minutes. Slice

251. Swedish Coffee Bread

Servings: 14 Slices
Cooking Time: 10 Minutes
Ingredients:
- 1 cup milk
- ½ tsp salt
- 1 egg yolk
- 2 Tbsp softened butter
- 3 cups all-purpose flour
- ⅓ cup sugar
- 1 envelope active dry yeast
- 3 tsp ground cardamom
- 2 egg whites, slightly beaten

Directions:
1. Preparing the Ingredients
2. Add each ingredient to the bread machine in the order and at the temperature recommended by your bread machine manufacturer.
3. Select the Bake cycle
4. Select the dough cycle and press start. Grease your baking sheet.
5. When the dough cycle has finished, divide the dough into three equal parts. Roll each part into a rope 12-14" long. Lay 3 ropes side by side, and then braid them together.
6. Tuck the ends underneath and put onto the sheet. Next, cover the bread, using kitchen towel, and let it rise until it has doubled in size. Brush your bread with beaten egg white and sprinkle with pearl sugar. Bake until golden brown at 375°F in a preheated oven for 20-25 minutes. When baked, remove the bread and put it on a cooling rack.

252. Cottage Cheese Bread

Servings: 1 Loaf
Cooking Time: 45 Minutes
Ingredients:
- 1/2 cup water
- 1 cup cottage cheese
- Two tablespoons margarine
- One egg
- One tablespoon white sugar
- 1/4 teaspoon baking soda
- One teaspoon salt
- 3 cups bread flour
- 2 1/2 teaspoons active dry yeast

Directions:
1. Into the bread machine, place the ingredients according to the ingredients list's order, then push the start button. In case the dough looks too sticky, feel free to use up to half a cup more bread flour.

Nutrition Info: Calories: 171 calories;Total Carbohydrate: 26.8 g ;Cholesterol: 18 mg ;Total Fat: 3.6 g ;Protein: 7.3 g ;Sodium: 324 mg

253. Honey Granola Bread

Servings: 1 Loaf
Cooking Time: 10 Minutes Plus Fermenting Time
Ingredients:
- 12 slice bread (1½ pounds)
- 1⅛ cups milk, at 80°F to 90°F
- 3 tablespoons honey
- 1½ tablespoons butter, melted and cooled
- 1⅛ teaspoons salt
- ¾ cup whole-wheat flour
- ⅔ cup prepared granola, crushed
- 1¾ cups white bread flour
- 1½ teaspoons bread machine or instant yeast

Directions:
1. Preparing the Ingredients.
2. Choose the size of loaf of your preference and then measure the ingredients.
3. Add all of the ingredients mentioned previously in the list.

4. Close the lid after placing the pan in the bread machine.
5. Select the Bake cycle
6. Turn on the bread machine. Select the Basic/White setting, select the loaf size, and the crust color. Press start.
7. When the cycle is finished, carefully remove the pan from the bread maker and let it rest.
8. Remove the bread from the pan, put in a wire rack to Cool about 5 minutes. Slice

254. Rich Cheddar Bread

Servings: 1 Loaf
Cooking Time: 10 Minutes Plus Fermenting Time
Ingredients:
- 12 slice bread (1½ pounds)
- 1 cup milk, at 80°F to 90°F
- 2 tablespoons butter, melted and cooled
- 3 tablespoons sugar
- 1 teaspoon salt
- ½ cup (2 ounces) grated aged Cheddar cheese
- 3 cups white bread flour
- 2 teaspoons bread machine or instant yeast

Directions:
1. Preparing the Ingredients.
2. Choose the size of loaf of your preference and then measure the ingredients.
3. Add all of the ingredients mentioned previously in the list.
4. Close the lid after placing the pan in the bread machine.
5. Select the Bake cycle
6. Turn on the bread machine. Select the Quick/Rapid setting, select the loaf size, and the crust color. Press start.
7. When the cycle is finished, carefully remove the pan from the bread maker and let it rest.
8. Remove the bread from the pan, put in a wire rack to Cool about 5 minutes. Slice

255. Simple Cottage Cheese Bread

Servings: 1 Loaf
Cooking Time: 10 Minutes Plus Fermenting Time
Ingredients:
- 12 slice bread (1½ pounds)
- ½ cup water, at 80°F to 90°F
- ¾ cup cottage cheese, at room temperature
- 1 egg, at room temperature
- 2 tablespoons butter, melted and cooled
- 1 tablespoon sugar
- 1 teaspoon salt
- ¼ teaspoon baking soda
- 3 cups white bread flour
- 2 teaspoons bread machine or instant yeast

Directions:
1. Preparing the Ingredients.
2. Choose the size of loaf of your preference and then measure the ingredients.
3. Add all of the ingredients mentioned previously in the list.
4. Close the lid after placing the pan in the bread machine.
5. Select the Bake cycle
6. Turn on the bread machine. Select the White/Basic setting, select the loaf size, and the crust color. Press start.
7. When the cycle is finished, carefully remove the pan from the bread maker and let it rest.
8. Remove the bread from the pan, put in a wire rack to Cool about 5 minutes. Slice

256. Sweet Applesauce Bread

Servings: 1 Loaf
Cooking Time: 10 Minutes Plus Fermenting Time
Ingredients:
- 12 slice bread (1½ pounds)
- ⅔ cup lukewarm milk
- ¼ cup unsweetened applesauce, at room temperature
- 1 tablespoon unsalted butter, melted
- 1 tablespoon sugar
- 1 teaspoon table salt
- ¼ cup quick oats
- 2¼ cups white bread flour
- ½ teaspoon ground cinnamon
- Pinch ground nutmeg
- 2¼ teaspoons bread machine yeast

Directions:
1. Preparing the Ingredients.
2. Choose the size of loaf of your preference and then measure the ingredients.
3. Add all of the ingredients mentioned previously in the list.
4. Close the lid after placing the pan in the bread machine.
5. Select the Bake cycle

6. Turn on the bread machine. Select the Quick/Rapid setting, select the loaf size, and the crust color. Press start.
7. When the cycle is finished, carefully remove the pan from the bread maker and let it rest.
8. Remove the bread from the pan, put in a wire rack to Cool about 5 minutes. Slice

257. Saffron And Tomato Bread

Servings: 10
Cooking Time: 3 Hours And 25 Minutes
Ingredients:
- Bread machine yeast - 1 tsp.
- Wheat bread flour - 2½ cups
- Panifarin - 1 tbsp.
- Salt - 1½ tsp.
- White sugar - 1½ tbsp.
- Olive oil - 2 tbsp.
- Tomatoes - 2 tbsp. dried and chopped
- Tomato paste - 1 tbsp.
- Firm cheese - ½ cup (cubes)
- Feta cheese - ½ cup
- Saffron/safflower - 1 pinch
- Serum - 1½ cups

Directions:
1. Add everything in the bread machine pan according to bread machine recommendations.
2. Select Basic and Medium crest.
3. Remove the bread when done.
4. Cool, slice, and serve.

Nutrition Info: (Per Serving): Calories: 260; Total Fat: 9.2 g; Saturated Fat: 4 g; Carbohydrates: 35.5 g; Cholesterol: 20 mg; Fiber: 1.3 g; Calcium: 27 mg; Sodium: 611 mg; Protein: 8.9 g

258. Fruit Bread

Servings: 12
Cooking Time: 3 Hours And 27 Minutes
Ingredients:
- Nondairy milk – 1 ¼ cups, warm
- Olive oil – 2 ½ tbsp.
- Granulated sugar – ¼ cup
- Salt – 1 ¼ tsp.
- White bread flour – 3 cups
- Ground nutmeg – ¾ tsp.
- Cinnamon – ½ tsp.
- Bread machine yeast – 1 ¼ tsp.
- Dried fruit – ½ cup

Directions:
1. Add everything (except the dried fruits) in the bread machine according to machine recommendations.
2. Select Sweetbread setting and press Start.
3. Add the dried fruit after the beep.
4. Remove the bread when done.
5. Cool, slice, and serve.

Nutrition Info: (Per Serving): Calories: 184; Total Fat: 3.7 g; Saturated Fat: 0.6 g; Carbohydrates: 34.2 g; Cholesterol: 0 mg; Fiber: 1.8 g; Calcium: 44 mg; Sodium: 260 mg; Protein: 4.3 g

BREAD FROM AROUND THE WORLD

259. White Chocolate Bread

Servings: 1 Loaf
Cooking Time: 2 Hours And 55 Minutes
Ingredients:
- ¼ cup warm water
- 1 cup warm milk
- 1 egg
- ¼ cup butter, softened
- 3 cups bread flour
- 2 tablespoons brown sugar
- 2 tablespoons white sugar
- 1 teaspoon salt
- 1 teaspoon ground cinnamon
- 1 (.25 ounce) package active dry yeast
- 1 cup white chocolate chips

Directions:
1. Place all ingredients (except the white chocolate chips) in the pan of the bread machine in the order recommended by the manufacturer.
2. Select cycle; press Start.
3. If your machine has a Fruit setting, add the white chocolate chips at the signal, otherwise you can do it about 5 minutes before the kneading cycle has finished.

Nutrition Info: Calories 277 ;Protein 6.6g;Carbohydrates 39g;Fat: 10.5g

260. Corn Poppy Seeds Sour Cream Bread

Servings: 1 Loaf (16 Slices)
Cooking Time: 1 Hour And 30 Minutes
Ingredients:
- 3½ cups all-purpose flour
- 1¾ cups of cornflour
- 5 ounces sour cream
- Two tablespoons corn oil
- Two teaspoons active dry yeast
- Two teaspoons salt
- 16 ¼ ounces lukewarm water
- poppy seeds for sprinkling

Directions:
1. Select the program of your bread machine to BASIC and choose the crust colour to MEDIUM.
2. Press START.
3. After the kneading brush the loaf with the water and sprinkle with poppy seeds.
4. Wait until the program completes.
5. When done, take the bucket out and let it cool for 5-10 minutes.
6. Shake the loaf from the pan and let cool for 30 minutes on a cooling rack.
7. Slice, serve and enjoy the taste of fragrant homemade bread.

Nutrition Info: Calories 223;Total Fat 4.8g;Saturated Fat 1.6g;Cholesterol 4g;Sodium 297mg;Total Carbohydrate 39.9g;Total Sugars 0.2g;Protein 5.2g

261. Greek Bread

Servings: 18
Cooking Time: 3 Hours And 25 Minutes
Ingredients:
- Milk – 1 cup
- Crumbled feta cheese – ½ cup
- Chopped pitted kalamata olives – 1/3 cup
- Water – 2 tbsp.
- Oil – 2 tsp.
- Bread flour – 3 cups
- Sugar – 1 tbsp.
- Dried rosemary – 1 tsp., crushed
- Salt – ½ tsp.
- Active dry yeast – 1 tsp.

Directions:
1. Add everything in the bread machine according to bread machine recommendations.
2. Select Basic White bread cycle.
3. Remove the bread when done.
4. Cool, slice, and serve.

Nutrition Info: (Per Serving): Calories: 110; Total Fat: 2 g; Saturated Fat: 0.5 g; Carbohydrates: 18 g; Cholesterol: 4 mg; Fiber: 1 g; Calcium: 38 mg; Sodium: 118 mg; Protein: 4 g

262. Spicy Bread

Servings: 6 Pcs
Cooking Time: 40 Minutes
Ingredients:
- ½ cup coconut flour
- Six eggs
- Three large jalapenos, sliced
- 4 ounces' turkey bacon, sliced
- ½ cup ghee
- ¼ tsp. baking soda

- ¼ tsp. salt
- ¼ cup of water

Directions:
1. Preheat the oven to 400F.
2. Cut bacon and jalapenos on a baking tray and roast for 10 minutes.
3. Flip and bake for five more minutes.
4. Remove seeds from the jalapenos.
5. Place jalapenos and bacon slices in a food processor and blend until smooth.
6. In a bowl, add ghee, eggs, and ¼-cup water. Mix well.
7. Then add some coconut flour, baking soda, and salt. Stir to mix.
8. Add bacon and jalapeno mix.
9. Grease the loaf pan with ghee.
10. Pour batter into the loaf pan.
11. Bake for 40 minutes.
12. Enjoy.

Nutrition Info: Calories: 240; Fat: 20g

263. European Black Bread

Servings: 1 Loaf
Cooking Time: 1 Hour And 5 Minutes
Ingredients:
- ¾ teaspoon cider vinegar
- 1 cup of water
- ½ cup rye flour
- 1 ½ cups flour
- One tablespoon margarine
- ¼ cup of oat bran
- One teaspoon salt
- 1 ½ tablespoons sugar
- One teaspoon dried onion flakes
- One teaspoon caraway seed
- One teaspoon yeast
- Two tablespoons unsweetened cocoa

Directions:
1. Put everything in your bread machine.
2. Now select the basic setting.
3. Hit the start button.
4. Transfer bread to a rack for cooling once done.

Nutrition Info: Calories 114; Carbohydrates: 22 g; Total Fat 1.7 g; Cholesterol 0mg; Protein 3 g; Sugar 2 g; Sodium 247 mg

264. Seeded Whole Wheat Bread

Servings: 1 Pound Loaf
Cooking Time: 3 Hours
Ingredients:
- Lukewarm water : ⅔ cups
- Milk powder : 3 tbsp
- Honey : 1 tbsp
- Unsalted butter, softened : 1 tbsp
- Plain bread flour : 1 cup
- Whole wheat flour : 1 cup
- Poppy seeds : 2 tbsp
- Sesame seeds : 2 tbsp
- Sunflower seeds : 2 tbsp
- Salt : ¾ tsp
- Instant dry yeast : 2 tsp

Directions:
1. Add the ingredients into the bread machine as per the order of the ingredients listed above or follow your bread machine's instruction manual.
2. Select the basic setting and medium crust function.
3. When ready, turn the bread out onto a drying rack and allow it to cool, then serve.

Nutrition Info: (Per Serving): Calories: 84 kcal / Total fat: 2 g / Saturated fat: 1 g / Cholesterol: 2 mg / Total carbohydrates: 14 g / Dietary fiber: 1 g Sodium: 133 mg / Protein: 3 g

265. Fluffy Paleo Bread

Servings: 15 Slices
Cooking Time: 40 Minutes
Ingredients:
- One ¼ cup almond flour
- Five eggs
- 1 tsp. lemon juice
- 1/3 cup avocado oil
- One dash black pepper
- ½ tsp. sea salt
- 3 to 4 tbsp. tapioca flour
- 1 to 2 tsp. Poppyseed
- ¼ cup ground flaxseed
- ½ tsp. baking soda
- Top with:
- Poppy seeds
- Pumpkin seeds

Directions:
1. Preheat the oven to 350F.
2. Line a baking pan with parchment paper and set aside.
3. In a bowl, add eggs, avocado oil, and lemon juice and whisk until combined.

4. In another bowl, add tapioca flour, almond flour, baking soda, flaxseed, black pepper, and poppy seed. Mix.
5. Add the lemon juice mixture into the flour mixture and mix well.
6. Add the batter into the prepared loaf pan and top with extra pumpkin seeds and poppy seeds.
7. Cover loaf pan and transfer into the prepared oven, and bake for 20 minutes. Remove cover and bake until an inserted knife comes out clean after about 15 to 20 minutes.
8. Remove from oven and cool.
9. Slice and serve.

Nutrition Info: Calories: 149 Cal;Fat: 12.9 g;Carbohydrates: 4.4 g

266. Peanut Butter And Jelly Bread

Servings: 1 Loaf
Cooking Time: 1 Hour And 10 Minutes
Ingredients:
- 1 1/2 tablespoons vegetable oil
- 1 cup of water
- ½ cup blackberry jelly
- ½ cup peanut butter
- One teaspoon salt
- One tablespoon white sugar
- 2 cups of bread flour
- 1 cup whole-wheat flour
- 1 1/2 teaspoons active dry yeast

Directions:
1. Put everything in your bread machine pan.
2. Select the basic setting.
3. Press the start button.
4. Take out the pan when done and set aside for 10 minutes.

Nutrition Info: Calories: 153 Cal;Carbohydrates: 20 g;Fat: 9g;Cholesterol: 0mg;Protein: 4g;Fiber: 2g ;Sugar: 11g;Sodium: 244mg;Potassium: 120mg

267. Quick Bake Italian Bread

Servings: 1 Pound Loaf
Cooking Time: 1 Hour And 20 Minutes
Ingredients:
- Lukewarm water :¾ cup
- Unsalted butter, softened :1 tbsp
- Plain bread flour :2 cups
- Powdered milk :1 ½ tbsp
- Dried marjoram :¾ tsp
- Dried basil :¾ tsp
- Dried thyme :½ tsp
- Salt :¼ tsp
- Sugar :1 ½ tbsp
- Instant dry yeast :2 tsp

Directions:
1. Add the ingredients into the bread machine as per the order of the ingredients listed above or follow your bread machine's instruction manual.
2. Select the quick or rapid setting and medium crust function.
3. When ready, turn the bread out onto a drying rack and allow it to cool, then serve.

Nutrition Info: (Per Serving):Calories: 126 kcal / Total fat: 3 g / Saturated fat: 1 g / Cholesterol: 6 mg / Total carbohydrates: 22 g / Dietary fiber: 1 g / Sodium: 109 mg / Protein: 4 g

268. Portuguese Sweet Bread

Servings: 1 Loaf
Cooking Time: 1 Hour And 5 Minutes
Ingredients:
- One egg beaten
- 1 cup milk
- 1/3 cup sugar
- Two tablespoons margarine
- 3 cups bread flour
- ¾ teaspoon salt
- 2 ½ teaspoons active dry yeast

Directions:
1. Place everything into your bread machine.
2. Select the sweet bread setting. Hit the start button.
3. Transfer the loaves to a rack for cooling once done.

Nutrition Info: Calories 139;Carbohydrates: 24 g;Total Fat 8.3 g;Cholesterol 14 mg;Protein 3 g;Fiber 0g;Sugar 4 g;Sodium 147 mg

269. Bacon And Cheese Bread

Servings: 1 Pound Loaf
Cooking Time: 3 Hours
Ingredients:
- Egg, lightly beaten :½
- Lukewarm water :½ cup
- Unsalted butter, diced :½ tbsp
- Shredded cheddar cheese :½ cup
- Bacon bits :2 tbsp
- Plain bread flour :2 cups
- Salt :½ tsp

- Sugar :1 tbsp
- Active dry yeast :1 tsp

Directions:
1. Add the ingredients into the bread machine as per the order of the ingredients listed above or follow your bread machine's instruction manual.
2. Select the basic cycle and light crust function.
3. When ready, turn the bread out onto a drying rack and allow it to cool, then serve.

Nutrition Info: (Per Serving):Calories: 171.3 kcal / Total fat: 4.6 g / Saturated fat: 2.5 g / Cholesterol: 26.9 mg / Total carbohydrates: 25.8 g / Dietary fiber: 1 g / Sodium: 283.1 mg / Protein: 6.2 g

270. Italian Panettone

Servings: 16
Cooking Time: 3 Hours
Ingredients:
- 3/4 cup warm water
- 4 large egg yolks
- 2 teaspoons vanilla extract
- 1/2 cup sugar
- 1 teaspoon lemon zest
- 1 teaspoon orange zest
- 1/2 teaspoon salt
- 1/2 cup unsalted butter, softened and cut into pieces
- 3 1/4 cups unbleached flour
- 1 package bread machine yeast
- 1/2 cup golden raisins
- 1/2 cup raisins
- 1 egg white, slightly beaten
- 4 sugar cubes, crushed

Directions:
1. Add the water, egg yolks, vanilla, and zest to the bread maker pan.
2. Add the sugar, salt, and flour.
3. Lay pieces of butter around the outside of the pan on top of the flour.
4. Press a well into the flour and add the yeast.
5. Start the Dough cycle; at the second kneading cycle add golden raisins and raisins.
6. Let dough rise until doubled.
7. Prepare the pan/baking case: cut a circle of parchment paper to line the bottom of the 6-inch cake pan and spray with non-stick cooking spray.
8. Cut another piece of parchment to line the inside of the brown paper bag after you have cut the bottom out of the bag.
9. Fold the top edge down to form a cuff then spray the inside of the parchment with cooking spray. Place the paper case in the pan.
10. Punch the dough down and knead into a ball.
11. Add it to the paper-lined pan case and allow to rise until almost doubled.
12. Preheat the oven to 350°F.
13. Baste the top of the panettone dough with the beaten egg white and sprinkle with the crushed sugar cubes.
14. Bake for 30 minutes, then reduce heat to 325°F and bake another 30 minutes.
15. Remove from oven and allow to cool in pan for about 15 minutes, then cool on a rack until ready to serve.

Nutrition Info: Calories: 201, Sodium: 120 mg, Dietary Fiber: 1 g, Fat: 7.2 g, Carbs: 30.6 g, Protein: 3.9 g

271. Peanut Butter Cookies

Servings: 12 Pcs
Cooking Time: 12 Minutes
Ingredients:
- 1 cup Peanut Butter(sugar-free)
- ½ cup Erythritol
- 1 Whole Egg

Directions:
1. Mix all ingredients into a bowl until it is combined.
2. Scoop the dough into a baking sheet lined with parchment. Press slightly to flatten.
3. Bake for 12 minutes.

Nutrition Info: Kcal per serve: 136;Fat: 12 g;Protein: 5 g;Carbs: 2g.

272. Country-styled White Bread

Servings: 1 Pound Loaf
Cooking Time: 2 Hours And 5 Minutes
Ingredients:
- Lukewarm water :1 ½ cups
- Extra-virgin olive oil :1 ½ tbsp
- Plain bread flour :1 cup
- White all-purpose Flour :2 ½ cups
- Baking soda :¼ tsp
- Sugar :1 ½ tsp
- Salt :1 pinch
- Bread machine yeast :2 ½ tsp

Directions:

1. Add the ingredients into the bread machine as per the order of the ingredients listed above or follow your bread machine's instruction manual.
2. Select the rapid setting and the medium crust function.
3. When ready, turn the bread out onto a drying rack and allow it to cool, then serve.

Nutrition Info: (Per Serving):Calories: 122 kcal / Total fat: 5 g / Saturated fat: 1 g / Cholesterol: 0 mg / Total carbohydrates: 17 g / Dietary fiber: 2 g Sodium: 394 mg / Protein: 2 g

273. Simple Dark Rye Bread

Servings: 1 Loaf (8 Slices)
Cooking Time: 2 Hours
Ingredients:
- 2/3 cup lukewarm water (80 degrees F)
- One tablespoon melted butter cooled
- ¼ cup molasses
- ¼ teaspoon salt
- One tablespoon unsweetened cocoa powder
- ½ cup rye flour
- pinch of ground nutmeg
- 1¼ cups white wheat flour sifted
- 1 1/8 teaspoons active dry yeast

Directions:
1. Prepare all of the ingredients for your bread and measuring means (a cup, a spoon, kitchen scales).
2. Carefully measure the ingredients into the pan.
3. Place all of the ingredients into the bread bucket in the right order and follow your bread machine's manual.
4. Close the cover.
5. Select the program of your bread machine to BASIC and choose the crust colour to MEDIUM.
6. Wait until the program completes.
7. When done, take the bucket out and let it cool for 5-10 minutes.
8. Shake the loaf from the pan and let cool for 30 minutes on a cooling rack.
9. Slice, serve and enjoy the taste of fragrant homemade bread.

Nutrition Info: Calories 151;Total Fat 2.1g;Saturated Fat 1g;Cholesterol 4g;Sodium 88mg;Total Carbohydrate 29.4g;Dietary Fiber 2.7g;Total Sugars 5.9g;Protein 4.2g

274. Oatmeal Bread

Servings: 1 Loaf (12 Slices)
Cooking Time: 3 Hours
Ingredients:
- 1½ teaspoon active dry yeast
- 2 cups (350 g) white bread flour, sifted
- ½ cup (100 g) oatmeal flour
- One teaspoon salt
- Two tablespoons liquid honey (can be replaced with sugar)
- ½ cup (150 ml) yogurt
- One tablespoon butter, melted
- ¾ cup (200 ml) lukewarm water (80 degrees F)
- Two tablespoons oatmeal flakes

Directions:
1. Prepare all of the ingredients for your bread and measuring means (a cup, a spoon, kitchen scales).
2. Carefully measure the ingredients into the pan.
3. Place all of the ingredients into a bread bucket in the right order and follow your bread machine's manual.
4. Close the cover.
5. Select the program of your bread machine to BASIC and choose the crust colour to MEDIUM.
6. Press START.
7. After the kneading lubricate the loaf's surface water or egg yolk and sprinkle with oat flakes.
8. Wait until the program completes.
9. When done, take the bucket out and let it cool for 5-10 minutes.
10. Shake the loaf from the pan and let cool for 30 minutes on a cooling rack.
11. Slice, serve and enjoy the taste of fragrant homemade bread.

Nutrition Info: Calories 176;Total Fat 2.3g;Saturated Fat 1.2g;Sodium 313mg;Total Carbohydrate 32.9g;Dietary Fiber 1.6g;Total Sugars 5.5g;Protein 5.5g

275. Amish Wheat Bread

Servings: 12
Cooking Time: 2 Hours 50 Minutes
Ingredients:
- 1 1/8 cups warm water
- 1 package active dry yeast
- 2 3/4 cups wheat flour
- 1/2 teaspoon salt
- 1/3 cup sugar

- 1/4 cup canola oil
- 1 large egg

Directions:
1. Add warm water, sugar and yeast to bread maker pan; let sit for 8 minutes or until it foams.
2. Add remaining ingredients to the pan.
3. Select Basic bread cycle, light crust color, and press Start.
4. Transfer to a cooling rack for 20 minutes before slicing.

Nutrition Info: Calories: 173, Sodium: 104 mg, Dietary Fiber: 0.9 g, Fat: 5.3 g, Carbs: 27.7 g, Protein: 3.7 g

276. Raisin Bread

Servings: 1 Pound Loaf
Cooking Time: 3 Hours
Ingredients:
- Lukewarm water :⅙ cup
- Unsalted butter, diced :1 ¼ tbsp
- Plain bread flour :2 cups
- Orange zest :1 pinch
- Ground cinnamon :1 ⅓ tsp
- Ground clove :1 pinch
- Ground nutmeg :1 pinch
- Salt :1 pinch
- Sugar :1 ¼ tbsp
- Active dry yeast :1 ½ tsp
- Raisins :½ cup

Directions:
1. Add the ingredients into the bread machine as per the order of the ingredients listed above or follow your bread machine's instruction manual. Do not add the raisins in yet.
2. Select the nut or raisin setting and medium crust function.
3. When the machine signals you to add the raisins, do so.
4. When ready, turn the bread out onto a drying rack and allow it to cool, then serve.

Nutrition Info: (Per Serving):Calories: 78 kcal / Total fat: 1 g / Saturated fat: 1 g / Cholesterol: 3m g / Total carbohydrates: 16 g / Dietary fiber: 1 g / Sodium: 106 mg / Protein: 2 g

277. Spiced Jalapeno Cheese Bread

Servings: 1 Pound Loaf
Cooking Time: 3 Hours
Ingredients:
- Lukewarm water :½ cup
- Milk powder :2 tbsp
- Unsalted butter :2 tbsp
- Plain bread flour :1 ½ cup
- Cheddar cheese :½ cup
- Jalapeno pepper, finely diced :½
- Granulated brown sugar :1 tbsp
- Salt :1 tsp
- Bread machine yeast :¾ tsp

Directions:
1. Combine the water and instant milk powder first, then add it to your bread machine.
2. Add the remaining ingredients into the bread machine as per the order of the ingredients listed above or follow your bread machine's instruction manual.
3. Select the basic setting and soft crust function.
4. When ready, turn the bread out onto a drying rack and allow it to cool, then serve.

Nutrition Info: (Per Serving):Calories: 135 kcal / Total fat: 4.9 g / Saturated fat: 3 g / Cholesterol: 14 mg / Total carbohydrates: 18.1 g / Dietary fiber: 0.7 g / Sodium: 327 mg / Protein: 4.6 g

278. Keto Breadsticks

Servings: 2 Pcs
Cooking Time: 15-20 Minutes
Ingredients:
- 1 ½ cup mozzarella cheese, shredded
- 1-ounce cream cheese
- ½ cup almond flour
- Three tablespoons coconut flour
- One egg
- ½ cup mozzarella cheese, shredded
- 1/3 cup parmesan cheese, shredded
- ¼ cup egg wash
- One teaspoon parsley, finely chopped

Directions:
1. Add the ingredients for the bread into the bread pan.
2. Put the bread machine on "Manual" or "Dough" mode.
3. After the cycles are finished, place the dough on a surface with a light dusting of flour.
4. Divide the dough into four and then divide each quarter again into 6.
5. Roll each piece until it is 8 inches long. Place the rolled dough on a greased baking sheet.
6. Brush over each piece with the egg wash.

7. Cover, and allow it to rise for 10 minutes.
8. Preheat the oven to 400F.
9. Spread half of the toppings on each piece.
10. Bake for 5 minutes before spreading the remaining toppings on the breadsticks.
11. Bake for another 10 minutes, or until the cheese has melted.
12. Remove it and then let it cool down on a wire rack.

Nutrition Info: Calories: 207;Carbohydrates: 7g;Fat: 14g;Protein: 13g

279. Paleo And Dairy-free Bread

Servings: 1 Pound Loaf
Cooking Time: 3 Hours
Ingredients:
- Flax meal :¼ cup
- Chia seeds :2 tbsp
- Coconut oil, melted :⅛ cup
- Egg :1 ½
- Almond milk :¼ cup
- Honey :½ tbsp
- Almond flour :1 cup
- Tapioca flour :⅔ cup
- Coconut flour :⅛ cup
- Salt :½ tsp
- Cream of tartar :1 tsp
- Bread machine yeast :1 tsp

Directions:
1. In a mixing bowl, combine one tablespoon of flax meal with the chia seeds. Stir in the water and set aside.
2. In a separate mixing bowl, pour in the melted coconut oil, eggs, almond milk, and honey. Whisk together. Followed by whisking in the flax meal and chia seed mixture. Pour this into the bread machine.
3. In a mixing bowl, combine the almond, tapioca, and coconut flour. Add the remainder of the flax meal and salt. Add in the cream of tartar and baking soda.
4. Pour the dry ingredients on top of the wet ingredients.
5. Finish by adding the yeast.
6. Select the whole wheat setting and medium crust function.
7. When ready, turn the bread out onto a drying rack and allow it to cool, then serve.

Nutrition Info: (Per Serving):Calories: 142 kcal / Total fat: 6.3 g / Saturated fat: 1.8g / Cholesterol: 34.9 mg / Total carbohydrates: 15.5 g / Dietary fiber: 4.4 g / Sodium: 236.8 mg / Protein: 4.1 g

280. Russian Black Bread

Servings: 1
Cooking Time: 3 Hours
Ingredients:
- 1 1/4 cups dark rye flour
- 2 1/2 cups unbleached flour
- 1 teaspoon instant coffee
- 2 tablespoons unsweetened cocoa powder
- 1 tablespoon whole caraway seeds
- 1/2 teaspoon dried minced onion
- 1/2 teaspoon fennel seeds
- 1 teaspoon sea salt
- 2 teaspoons active dry yeast
- 1 1/3 cups water, at room temperature
- 1 teaspoon sugar
- 1 1/2 tablespoons dark molasses
- 1 1/2 tablespoons apple cider vinegar
- 3 tablespoons vegetable oil

Directions:
1. Mix dry ingredients together in a bowl, except for yeast.
2. Add wet ingredients to bread pan first; top with dry ingredients.
3. Make a well in the center of the dry ingredients and add the yeast.
4. Select Basic bread cycle, medium crust color, and press Start.
5. Let cool for 15 minutes before slicing.

Nutrition Info: Calories: 169, Sodium: 147 mg, Dietary Fiber: 3.9 g, Fat: 3.9 g, Carbs: 29.8 g, Protein: 4.6 g

281. Classic French Bread

Servings: 1 Pound Loaf
Cooking Time: 3 Hours
Ingredients:
- Lukewarm water :1 cup
- Sugar :2 tsp
- Salt :1 tsp
- Plain bread flour :3 ¼ cups
- Bread machine yeast :1 tsp

Directions:
1. Add the ingredients into the bread machine as per the order of the ingredients listed above or follow your bread machine's instruction manual.

2. Select the French setting and medium crust function.
3. When ready, turn the bread out onto a drying rack and allow it to cool, then serve.
Nutrition Info: (Per Serving):Calories: 206 kcal / Total fat: 0.6 g / Saturated fat: 0.1 g / Cholesterol: 0 mg Total carbohydrates: 43.4 g / Dietary fiber: 1.8 g Sodium: 292.2 mg / Protein: 5.9 g

282. Thin Crust Pizza Dough

Servings: 1 Pizza
Cooking Time: 1 Hour And 30 Minutes
Ingredients:
- Warm water – ¾ cup, 100°F to 110°F
- All-purpose flour – 2 cups
- Salt – ½ tsp.
- White sugar – ¼ tsp.
- Active dry yeast – 1 tsp.
- Olive oil 2 tsp.

Directions:
1. Add everything in the bread machine according to bread machine recommendations.
2. Select dough setting and start.
3. Transfer the dough to a well-floured work surface when done.
4. Roll the dough out into a thin crust and bake.
Nutrition Info: (Per Serving): Calories: 126.2; Total Fat: 1.5 g; Saturated Fat: 0.2 g; Carbohydrates: 24.2 g; Cholesterol: 0 mg; Fiber: 0.9 g; Calcium: 5.8 mg; Sodium: 146.9 mg; Protein: 3.4 g

283. Low-carb Zucchini Loaf

Servings: 1 Loaf
Cooking Time: 1 Hour And 30 Minutes
Ingredients:
- Two ¼ cup almond flour
- 1 ½ cup zucchini, grated
- ¾ cup no-calorie sweetener of your choice
- ½ cup walnuts, chopped
- ½ cup pecans, chopped
- Two tablespoons coconut flour
- Three teaspoons baking powder
- One teaspoon ground cinnamon
- ¼ teaspoon nutmeg
- ¼ teaspoon ginger, grated
- Five eggs, beaten
- ½ cup of coconut oil
- Two teaspoons vanilla extract

Directions:
1. First, put the wet ingredients into the pan, followed by all dry ingredients.
2. Press the "Quick" or "Cake" mode of your bread machine.
3. Allow the machine to complete all the cycles.
4. Take out the pan from the machine, but keep the loaf in the pan for another 10 minutes.
5. Remove the loaf from the pan to let it cool down faster.
6. Slice and serve.
Nutrition Info: Calories: 217;Carbohydrates: 5g;Fat: 15g;Protein: 5g

284. Italian Parmesan Bread

Servings: 1 Pound Loaf
Cooking Time: 3 Hours
Ingredients:
- Lukewarm water :¾ cups
- White all-purpose flour :2 cups
- Shredded parmesan cheese :⅛ cup
- Salt :¾ tsp
- Italian mixed herbs :½ tsp
- Garlic powder :½ tsp
- Instant dry yeast :1 ¼ tsp

Directions:
1. Add the ingredients into the bread machine as per the order of the ingredients listed above or follow your bread machine's instruction manual.
2. Select the basic setting and medium crust function.
3. When ready, turn the bread out onto a drying rack and allow it to cool, then serve.
Nutrition Info: (Per Serving):Calories: 103.1 kcal / Total fat: 0.4 g / Saturated fat: 0.1 g / Cholesterol: 0.2 mg / Total carbohydrates: 21.3 g / Dietary fiber: 0.8 g / Sodium: 14.1 g / Protein: 3 g

285. Milk White Bread

Servings: 1 Loaf
Cooking Time: 3 Hours And 30 Minutes
Ingredients:
- 1¼ cups (280 ml / 9½ oz.) Lukewarm whole milk
- 5¼ cups (680 g) wheat bread machine flour
- 2 tbsp. vegetable oil
- 2 tbsp. sour cream
- 2 tsp. bread machine yeast
- 1 tbsp. white sugar

- 2 tsp. salt

Directions:
1. Place all the dry and liquid ingredients in the pan and follow the instructions for your bread machine.
2. Pay particular attention to measuring the ingredients. Use a cup, measuring spoon, and
3. kitchen scales to do so.
4. Set the baking program to BASIC also set the crust type to MEDIUM.
5. If the dough is too wet, adjust the
6. After mixing the dough thoroughly, smear the surface of the merchandise with soured cream.
7. When the program has ended, take the pan out of the bread machine and cool for five minutes.
8. Shake the loaf out of the pan. If necessary, use a spatula.
9. Wrap the bread with a kitchen towel and set it aside for an hour or, you can make it cool on a wire rack.
10. Cool, serve, and luxuriate.

Nutrition Info: Calories 344;Total Fat 4.9g;Saturated Fat 1.2g;Cholesterol 1g;Carbohydrate 64.6g;Total Sugars 1.7g;Protein 8.9g

286. Puri Bread

Servings: 6 Pcs
Cooking Time: 5 Minutes
Ingredients:
- 1 cup almond flour, sifted
- ½ cup of warm water
- 2 Tbsp. clarified butter
- 1 cup olive oil for frying
- Salt to taste

Directions:
1. Salt the water and add the flour.
2. Make some holes in the center of the dough and pour warm clarified butter.
3. Knead the dough and let stand for 15 minutes, covered.
4. Shape into six balls.
5. Flatten the balls into six thin rounds using a rolling pin.
6. Heat enough oil to cover a round frying pan completely.
7. Place a puri in it when hot.
8. Fry for 20 seconds on each side.
9. Place on a paper towel.
10. Repeat with the rest of the puri and serve.

Nutrition Info: Calories: 106;Fat: 3g;Carb: 6g;Protein: 3g

287. Sausage Bread

Servings: 10
Cooking Time: 3 Hours And 25 Minutes
Ingredients:
- Bread machine yeast – 1 tsp.
- Wheat bread machine flour – 3 ½ cups
- Kosher salt – 1 tsp.
- Sugar – 1 tbsp.
- Olive oil – 1 ½ tbsp.
- Smoked sausage – 2 tbsp., chopped into small cubes
- Grated cheddar cheese – 2 tbsp., grated
- Garlic – 1 tbsp., crushed
- Lukewarm water – 1 cup

Directions:
1. Add everything (except the sausage) in the bread machine according to bread machine recommendations.
2. Select Basic cycle and Medium crust.
3. Add the sausage after the beep.
4. Remove the bread when done.
5. Cool, slice and serve.

Nutrition Info: (Per Serving): Calories: 260; Total Fat: 5.6 g; Saturated Fat: 1.4 g; Carbohydrates: 43.8 g; Cholesterol: 8 mg; Fiber: 1.6 g; Calcium: 55 mg; Sodium: 355 mg; Protein: 7.7 g

288. Ciabatta

Servings: 1 Pound Loaf
Cooking Time: 30 Minutes
Ingredients:
- Lukewarm water :¾ cup
- Extra-virgin olive oil :½ tbsp
- White all-purpose flour :1 ½ cups
- Salt :¾ tsp
- Sugar :½ tsp
- Bread machine yeast :¾ tsp

Directions:
1. Add the ingredients into the bread machine as per the order of the ingredients listed above or follow your bread machine's instruction manual.
2. Select the dough cycle.
3. When the dough is ready, place it onto a floured surface. Cover the dough with a ceramic or glass dish and allow it to rest for ten minutes.

4. Shape the dough an oval shape. Split into two oval shapes when doubling up on the recipe.
5. Place onto a greased baking tray, cover with a cloth and allow to rest for a further 30 minutes or until it has doubled in size. Allow the dough to rest in a dry, warm area of your kitchen.
6. Preheat your oven to 425 ℉.
7. Using the bottom end of a wooden spoon make small indents on the top of each loaf. Drive the spoon down into the dough until it touches the baking tray. Then place into the oven and bake for 30 minutes.
8. Sprinkle water lightly over the top of the loaves every 10 minutes while baking.
9. When ready, turn the bread out onto a drying rack and allow it to cool, then serve.

Nutrition Info: (Per Serving):Calories: 190 kcal / Total fat: 2.2 g / Saturated fat: 0.3 g / Cholesterol: 0 mg / Total carbohydrates: 36.6 g / Dietary fiber: 1.4 g / Sodium: 441 mg / Protein: 5.1 g

289. Syrian Bread

Servings: 8 Pcs
Cooking Time: 20 Minutes
Ingredients:
- Two tablespoons vegetable oil
- 1 cup of water
- 1 ½ teaspoons salt
- ½ teaspoon white sugar
- 1 ½ teaspoon active dry yeast
- 3 cups all-purpose flour

Directions:
1. Put everything in your bread machine pan.
2. Select the dough cycle. Hit the start button.
3. Preheat your oven to 475 degrees F.
4. Turn to dough on a lightly floured surface once done.
5. Divide it into eight equal pieces. Form them into rounds.
6. Take a damp cloth and cover the rounds with it.
7. Now roll the dough into flat thin circles. They should have a diameter of around 8 inches.
8. Cook in your preheated baking sheets until they are golden brown and puffed.

Nutrition Info: Calories 204;Carbohydrates: 36g;Total Fat 5g;Cholesterol 0mg;Protein 5g;Fiber 1g;Sugar 0g;Sodium 438mg;Potassium 66mg

290. Corn Bread

Servings: 1 Loaf
Cooking Time: 3 Hours And 30 Minutes
Ingredients:
- 3½ cups (480 g) cornflour
- 1½ cups (200 g) bread machine wheat flour, sifted
- 2 tbsp. butter softened
- ½ cup cornflakes
- 1 tbsp. white sugar
- 2 tsp. Bread machine yeast
- 2 tsp. salt

Directions:
1. Place all the dry and liquid ingredients in the pan and follow the instructions for your bread machine.
2. Pay particular attention to measuring the ingredients. Use a cup, measuring spoon, and kitchen scales to do so.
3. Set the baking program to primary also set the crust type to medium.
4. If the dough is too wet, adjust the recipe's flour and liquid quantity.
5. After mixing the dough thoroughly, moisten the merchandise's surface with water and sprinkle with cornflakes.
6. When the program has ended, take the pan out of the bread machine and cool for five minutes.
7. Shake the loaf out of the pan. If necessary, use a spatula.
8. Wrap the bread with a kitchen towel and set it aside for an hour. Otherwise, you'll calm on a wire rack.

Nutrition Info: Calories 319;Total Fat 5.1g;saturated fat 2.1g;Cholesterol 8g;Sodium 634mg;Carbohydrate 62.3g;dietary fibre 4.8g;total sugars 2.1g;Protein 7.3g

291. Vanilla Milk Bread

Servings: 1 Loaf
Cooking Time: 3 Hours And 30 Minutes
Ingredients:
- 4½ cups (580 g) wheat bread machine flour
- 1¾ cups (370 ml / 12½ oz.) lukewarm whole milk
- 1 tbsp. white sugar
- One packet vanilla sugar
- 2 tbsp. extra-virgin olive oil
- 2 tsp. bread machine yeast

- 2 tsp. sea salt

Directions:
1. Place all the dry and liquid ingredients in the pan and follow the instructions for your bread machine.
2. Pay particular attention to measuring the ingredients. Use a cup, measuring spoon, and kitchen scales to do so.
3. Set, the baking program to BASIC, also set the crust type to MEDIUM.
4. If the dough is too wet, adjust the recipe's flour and liquid quantity.
5. When the program has ended, take the pan out of the bread machine and cool for five minutes.
6. Shake the loaf out of the pan. If necessary, use a spatula.
7. Wrap the bread with a kitchen towel and set it aside for an hour. Otherwise, you'll calm on a wire rack.

Nutrition Info: Calories 328;Total Fat 5.7g;Saturated Fat 1.4g;Cholesterol 4g;Sodium 610mg;Carbohydrate 59.1g;Dietary Fiber 2.1g;Total Sugars 4.6g;Protein 9.4g

292. Low-carb Apple Bread

Servings: 1 Loaf
Cooking Time: 1 Hour And 30 Minutes
Ingredients:
- Two apples, peeled and chopped
- 2 cups almond flour
- ½ cup golden flaxseed, milled
- ½ cup no-calorie sweetener of your choice
- Two teaspoons cinnamon
- ¾ teaspoon baking soda
- ¾ teaspoon salt
- ½ teaspoon nutmeg
- Four eggs, lightly beaten
- ¼ cup of water
- ¼ cup heavy cream
- Four tablespoons coconut oil
- Two teaspoons vanilla extract
- 1 ½ teaspoon apple cider vinegar

Directions:
1. Place all ingredients in the pan according to the order specified above.
2. Set the bread machine to "Cake" or "Quick" mode.
3. Let the cycles finish.
4. Remove the bread pan from the machine, but keep the bread in the pan for another 10 minutes.
5. Slice the bread only when it has cooled down.

Nutrition Info: Calories: 242;Carbohydrates: 11g;Fat: 20g;Protein: 7g

293. Soft Pretzels

Servings: 24 Pcs
Cooking Time: 20 Minutes
Ingredients:
- oz. cocoa butter
- ½ cup coconut butter
- ½ cup sugar-free maple syrup
- 1/3 cup heavy cream
- 3 tbsp coconut oil
- Two scoops matcha MCT powder
- 2 tsp vanilla essence

Directions:
1. Start by throwing all the ingredients into a saucepan.
2. Stir cook on low heat until butter is melted, then stir well.
3. Spread this mixture in an 8x8-inch pan lined with parchment paper.
4. Refrigerate for 3 hours, then slice into 24 pieces.

Nutrition Info: Calories 173;Total Fat 13 g;Saturated Fat 10.1 g;Cholesterol 12 mg;Sodium 67 mg;Total Carbs 7.5 g;Sugar 1.2 g;Fibre 0.6 g;Protein 3.2 g

294. Pita Bread

Servings: 8 Pcs
Cooking Time: 20 Minutes
Ingredients:
- 3 cups of all-purpose flour
- 1 1/8 cups warm water
- One tablespoon of vegetable oil
- One teaspoon salt
- 1 ½ teaspoon active dry yeast
- One active teaspoon white sugar

Directions:
1. Place all the ingredients in your bread pan.
2. Select the dough setting. Hit the start button.
3. The machine beeps after the dough rises adequately.
4. Turn the dough on a floured surface.
5. Roll and stretch the dough gently into a 12-inch rope.

6. Cut into eight pieces with a knife.
7. Now roll each piece into a ball. It should be smooth.
8. Roll each ball into a 7-inch circle. Keep covered with a towel on a floured top for 30 minutes for the pita to rise. It should get puffy slightly.
9. Preheat your oven to 260 degrees C.
10. Keep the pitas on your wire cake rack. Transfer to the oven rack directly.
11. Bake the pitas for 5 minutes. They should be puffed. The top should start to brown.
12. Take out from the oven. Keep the pitas immediately in a sealed paper bag. You can also cover using a damp kitchen towel.
13. Split the top edge or cut into half once the pitas are soft. You can also have the whole pitas if you want.

Nutrition Info: Calories 191;Carbohydrates: 37g;Total Fat 3g;Cholesterol 0mg;Protein 5g;Fiber 1g;Sugar 1g;Sodium 293mg;Potassium 66mg

295. German Pumpernickel Bread

Servings: 1 Loaf
Cooking Time: 1 Hour And 10 Minutes
Ingredients:
- 1 1/2 tablespoon vegetable oil
- 1 1/8 cups warm water
- Three tablespoons cocoa
- 1/3 cup molasses
- 1 ½ teaspoons salt
- One tablespoon caraway seeds
- 1 cup rye flour
- 1 ½ cups of bread flour
- 1 ½ tablespoon wheat gluten
- 1 cup whole wheat flour
- 2 ½ teaspoons bread machine yeast

Directions:
1. Put everything in your bread machine.
2. Select the primary cycle.
3. Hit the start button.
4. Transfer bread to a rack for cooling once done.

Nutrition Info: Calories 119;Carbohydrates: 22.4 g;Total Fat 2.3 g;Cholesterol 0mg;Protein 3 g;Sodium 295 mg

296. Fiji Sweet Potato Bread

Servings: 1 Loaf
Cooking Time: 1 Hour And 10minutes
Ingredients:
- One teaspoon vanilla extract
- ½ cup of warm water
- 4 cups flour
- 1 cup sweet mashed potatoes
- Two tablespoons softened butter
- ½ teaspoon cinnamon
- 1 ½ teaspoons salt
- 1/3 cup brown sugar
- Two tablespoons powdered milk
- Two teaspoons yeast

Directions:
1. Add everything in the pan of your bread.
2. Select the white bread and the crust you want.
3. Hit the start button.
4. Set aside on wire racks for cooling before slicing.

Nutrition Info: Calories: 168 Cal;Carbohydrates: 28 g;Fat: 5g;Cholesterol: 0 mg;Protein: 4 g;Fiber: 1g;Sugat 3 g;Sodium: 292 mg

297. Pita Bread With Black Cumin

Servings: 8 Pcs
Cooking Time: 15 Minutes
Ingredients:
- 2 cups almond flour, sifted
- ½ cup of water
- 2 Tbsp. olive oil
- Salt, to taste
- 1 tsp. black cumin

Directions:
1. Preheat the oven to 400F.
2. Combine the flour with salt. Add the water and olive oil.
3. Knead the dough and let stand about 15 minutes.
4. Shape the dough into eight balls.
5. Line a baking sheet with parchment paper and flatten the balls into eight thin rounds.
6. Sprinkle black cumin.
7. Bake for 15 minutes, serve.

Nutrition Info: Calories: 73;Fat: 6.9g;Carbohydrates: 1.6g;Protein: 1.6g

298. Gluten-free Bread

Servings: 1 Pound Loaf
Cooking Time: 2 Hours And 35 Minutes
Ingredients:
- Lukewarm water :1 ⅛ cups
- Unsalted butter, diced :⅛ cup

- Egg :1 ½
- Apple cider vinegar :¾ tsp
- Honey :⅓ cup
- Gluten-free, all-purpose flour :2 ¼ cups
- Salt :¾ tsp
- Xanthan gum :1 ⅛ tsp
- Bread machine yeast :1 ⅛ tsp

Directions:
1. Add the ingredients into the bread machine as per the order of the ingredients listed above or follow your bread machine's instruction manual.
2. Select the basic setting and soft crust function.
3. When ready, turn the bread out onto a drying rack and allow it to cool, then serve.

Nutrition Info: (Per Serving):Calories: 212 kcal / Total fat: 6g / Saturated fat: 3g / Cholesterol: 40 mg / Total carbohydrates: 35 g / Dietary fiber: 3 g Sodium: 263 mg / Protein: 5 g

299. Coffee Cake

Servings: 8
Cooking Time: 1 Hour And 30 Minutes
Ingredients:
- • Yolk of one egg
- • ¾ cup whole milk
- • 1 tbsp unsalted butter, melted
- • 2 ¼ cups plain bread flour
- • ¼ cup sugar
- • 1 tsp salt
- • 2 tsp active dry yeast
- for glaze topping:
- • ¼ cup pecan nuts
- • ¼ cup walnuts
- • 1 tsp ground cinnamon
- • ½ cup sugar
- • 2 tbsp unsalted butter, melted

Directions:
1. Add the ingredients into the bread machine as per the order of the ingredients listed above or follow your bread machine's instruction manual.
2. Select the dough setting.
3. Prepare a 8 x 8" baking pan by greasing it.
4. When the dough cycle is finished, transfer the cake dough into the greased baking pan.
5. For the topping, glaze the two tablespoons of melted butter over the top.
6. In a small mixing bowl, combine the nuts, sugar, and cinnamon and sprinkle over the top of the cake dough.
7. Cover the cake dough with a cloth and allow to rest in a warm area for 30 minutes.
8. Preheat your oven to 375 ℉ and bake the cake for 20 minutes or until it has turned a golden color.
9. When ready, turn the bread out onto a drying rack and allow it to cool, then serve.

Nutrition Info: (Per Serving):Calories: 313.1 kcal / Total fat: 11.1 g / Saturated fat: 4 g / Cholesterol: 35.9 mg / Total carbohydrates: 48.5 g / Dietary fiber: 2 g / Sodium: 344.1 mg / Protein: 5.9 g

300. Argentine Chimichurri Bread

Servings: 15
Cooking Time: 3 Hours And 25 Minutes
Ingredients:
- Water – 1 cup
- White wine vinegar – 1 ½ tbsp.
- Olive oil – 3 tbsp.
- Cayenne pepper – 1/8 tsp.
- Dried oregano – ¾ tsp.
- Garlic – 2 cloves, minced
- Chopped onion – 3 tbsp.
- Fresh parsley – 3 tbsp.
- Salt – 1 ½ tsp.
- White sugar – 1 tbsp.
- Wheat bran – 3 tbsp.
- Bread flour – 3 cups
- Active dry yeast – 2 tsp.

Directions:
1. Place everything in the bread machine according to bread machine recommendations.
2. Select Basic or White cycle. Press Start.
3. Remove the bread when done.
4. Cool, slice, and serve.

Nutrition Info: (Per Serving): Calories: 32.5; Total Fat: 2.8 g; Saturated Fat: 0.4 g; Carbohydrates: 1.9 g; Cholesterol: 0 mg; Fiber: 0.5 g; Calcium: 4.6 mg; Sodium: 233.5 mg; Protein: 0.4 g

Made in the USA
Las Vegas, NV
20 August 2025